MATTERS
OF THE
HEART

MATTERS OF THE HEART

Healing Your Relationship with
Yourself and Those You Love

THEMA BRYANT, PhD

A TarcherPerigee Book

tarcherperigee

an imprint of Penguin Random House LLC
1745 Broadway, New York, NY 10019
penguinrandomhouse.com

TarcherPerigee with tp colophon is a registered trademark of Penguin Random House LLC

Most TarcherPerigee books are available at special quantity discounts for bulk purchase for sales promotions, premiums, fundraising, and educational needs. Special books or book excerpts also can be created to fit specific needs. For details, write SpecialMarkets@ penguinrandomhouse.com.

Library of Congress Cataloging-in-Publication Data has been applied for.
ISBN 9780593719145 (hardcover)
ISBN 9780593719169 (ebook)

Printed in the United States of America
10 9 8 7 6 5 4 3 2 1

Book design by Angie Boutin

The authorized representative in the EU for product safety and compliance is Penguin Random House Ireland, Morrison Chambers, 32 Nassau Street, Dublin D02 YH68, Ireland https://eu-contact.penguin.ie.

This is a work of nonfiction. Some names and identifying details have been changed.

To my mother, Rev. Cecelia Williams Bryant,
who taught me the sacred fire of the heart for God, self,
and others.
You show me daily what it means to love fiercely,
unconditionally, and unapologetically.
My love for you transcends space and time.

These pages are also for each healing heart who dares to
show up authentically in this space.
May your new chapter bring clarity, rest, breath,
and love from within you and around you.
You're worthy.

CONTENTS

III.
HEALING RELATIONSHIP WOUNDS

IV.
CONCLUSION

MATTERS
OF THE
HEART

WHY YOUR HEART MATTERS

Peace and blessings to you, my sacred siblings. I am so glad you were intentional about starting this book and, more important, continuing the journey of attending to your heart. I come to this work as your facilitator—someone who has experienced living with a full heart, living a busy life with a neglected heart, going through the deep-sea diving of living with a broken heart, and tenderly and compassionately healing my heart. I'm so glad something about this title and topic called out to you.

You may have had years of your life where loss and disappointment were constant companions. You may have spent a childhood seeing people misuse, abuse, control, dominate, and manipulate others in the name of love. Perhaps you know what it's like to feel unloved or are uncertain how to give, receive, or maintain love. On the other hand, you may love deeply and love well, while being well-loved in return, and simply would like to continue to build your secure foundation. If any of this sounds like you, then you're reading the right book.

Some of you may come to this season of your lives and have minimal experiences with loving relationships. Your relationships or "situationships" may have been briefly satisfying or long-term and unhealthy. You may have been taught, directly or indirectly, to spend all of your time, energy, and money on your academic and vocational accomplishments. You may have invested in your skills training, education, work goals, and business plan. You may even have success in those areas, which is wonderful, yet there are aspects of you that are dissatisfied, even traumatized. The root of this human desire for *more* is the foundation of matters of the heart.

Finally, some of you may have been taught to take care of everyone and everything else but have not cultivated mutually caring, loving relationships. You may take care of family, friends, coworkers, and community members but have not experienced reciprocity, where you feel seen, heard, understood, supported, and cared for. The health of your heart is not just about your ability to give, sacrifice, pour out, and enrich others. A healthy heart has outward and inward flow. The inward flow is not only self-love but also the love of others, not just symbolically but tangibly. I invite you to take a breath and read that again.

Matters of the heart are inclusive of your relationship with yourself and others. When it comes to others, contemplate the nature of the different relationships in your life. Do you usually have a loving, romantic partner but have strained or nonexistent relationships with your family? Are you close to your family but have never been able to sustain friendships? Do you have lots of good friends but have not had a lasting loving intimate relationship? Which type of relationships have been ever present and which have been elusive? Do you tend to love yourself but isolate yourself and sabotage your connections with others, or do you chase the love of others to the point that you abandon yourself? To heal, you need to hear your heartbeat—the language, habits, movements, tendencies, rhythms, and journey of your heart.

I invite you to begin this journey with a reflection on love. When have you felt love? How did you recognize it? From whom have you felt it? What happened to your heart, and why in this moment have you chosen or been nudged to take this journey into it? Self-awareness and reflection are major parts of attending to the heart. This process is not merely about my sharing what I have learned from my life, science, practice, culture, and faith. This process is about coming to fuller awareness and activation of the wisdom you carry within your own heart.

There are many known benefits of healthy, loving relationships and many costs of loneliness and unhealthy relationships. For example:

- People with higher rates of self-love also have higher self-esteem, self-acceptance, and overall mental well-being. They enjoy healthier relationships, practice healthy boundary setting, and exhibit greater self-compassion, confidence, and self-care (regarding nutrition and exercise). They show energy, resilience, and determination, as well as less anxiety and stress.
- Benefits of healthy, loving social support include improved physical health and emotional well-being, a faster recovery from illness, healthier behaviors, a greater sense of purpose, and a longer life. Those who have a good support system experience less stress, depression, and post-traumatic stress disorder.
- In a recent report on the mental health crisis of loneliness in the United States, the surgeon general noted that loneliness is associated with substance abuse, social anxiety, cardiovascular disease, higher rates of mortality, depression, cognitive decline, perceived stress, and anger.
- If you remain in an unhealthy relationship due to fear of loneliness or for other reasons, the negative effects

may include but are not limited to depression, anxiety, PTSD, dissatisfaction, stress, and physical injury.

If you are on a relationship break because of hurt and disappointment, take into account that the reason you picked up this book is that a part of you still desires connection. Tuck these gems away for when you feel ready to open up to the possibility of new or revived connections. You will know when your heart is ready. View it as a breakthrough or progress when you shift from a firm *never* to a *maybe.* Your heart is healing and you are preparing to show back up for love.

Let me say that while I am glad that you have begun this book, it is my deep hope that you will read it to the end and apply what you learn and rediscover so you can live a more abundant life. While heartbreak, confusion, loneliness, or curiosity may have brought you here, I hope you will not shift your attention from your heart and stop reading before you complete the process. I know you have many life demands that pull on your time and attention, but your heart needs you. Your heart has been craving this attention for some time now. It's time to center your heart by heeding this momentous call to heal and grow. I also invite you to prepare for the journey by deciding if there is a certain place you would like to sit, a certain scent or tea that would support your process, and a specific journal or note-taking app you want to use to capture your reflections that exceed the space provided on these pages.

Along with being a clinical licensed psychologist, I am an ordained minister, so I approach the heart holistically. Interwoven in this book are both research findings and sacred insights. I hope you will give yourself permission to give both of those weight while also trusting the weight of your own wisdom. You have the option to accept, reject, or modify everything you read here to fit your circumstances. Some statements will resonate with you immediately, some will have a delayed impact that leaves you reflecting for a while, and some simply won't apply. These are all key aspects of digesting knowledge. My ultimate question is not whether you liked the book but if you uncovered or recovered something that helped your heart to heal and your life to be more fulfilling.

I also want to share with you I, too, have experienced a range of heart experiences that allow me to approach this work not just clinically or in a scholarly fashion but as someone who has known intimately what it is to desire love, to fall in love, to grow in love, to experience heartache, to heal my heart, and to choose to love again and again, both myself and others. So when I say, "I see you," I am not sitting across from you with a clipboard and a diagnosis at the ready, but rather am sitting alongside you with compassion for the seasons of everything falling apart and the seasons of rebuilding. You're worthy of all of that. Take as much time as you need. Anything less would be heartless. Rushing through this book would be heartless. Let's be heart-full together. In a world that tells us to silence ourselves, overwork ourselves, dissect ourselves, and shame ourselves, loving ourselves wholly and holy is a radical, revolutionary, sacred, delicious act. I celebrate that you are rejecting the lies that tell you to treat yourself as a heartless machine intended merely for labor and productivity. That's absolutely not who you are. You are a heart and a living soul. Get into it. Lean into it. Own it. Living heartfully looks good on you.

I wrote this book to take you through the journey of self-love and then love of others. I also recognize that you are an independent, thinking being, so you may scan the table of contents and choose to read any of the chapters first. If your life experiences cause a particular chapter to call to you, I understand *and* I still hope you will read or listen to the entire book in the order that aligns with you.

In fact, noting what calls to you and what doesn't can help you become more aware of yourself. Are you drawn to self-love material but shut down about matters of relational love? Do you read everything you can find about relationships while neglecting your inner garden? You don't have to choose. It is neither a fight nor a choice between love of self and love of others. When we are living in loving flow, that compassion pours inward and outward. I hope you open yourself up for both. You are worthy. As I received the download of inspiration for this book, I intentionally wrote it to take you from exploring self-love and relational love to healing and addressing relational challenges. This process can be thought of as a homecoming, which is the key concept of my podcast and first book. A homecoming is a reclaiming of yourself after stress and trauma may have disconnected you from yourself. If you have been disconnected from yourself, from your heart, from emotional availability or from relational love, this journey is for you.

You may wonder why a professor and researcher would write a book for you. An understanding of population health, liberation psychology, and womanist psychology bring me here. From population health, I recognize that the mental health system is broken and that mental health professionals are seeing only a small fraction of those who are suffering. Psychologists must not wait to see who will show up in our offices with the resources to access care but must intentionally design interventions that allow us to permeate the cultural landscape with knowledge that can enhance people's lives. From the vantage point of liberation psychology, I am clear that we need to challenge those structures that harm our hearts and cultivate communities based in that radical love, that regardless love, that love that defies stereotypes and biases. Finally, from the vantage point of womanist psychology, holistic wellness wisdom from Black women, I understand that our hearts are integral to who we are in relationship to ourselves and to each other. To flourish, I invite you to honor and integrate your heart.

I wrote this book for you, those of you who proclaim boldly that you love yourself and always have, those of you who acknowledge that it has been a struggle but you are now at a place of self-love, and those of you who find the idea of loving yourself difficult if not impossible. You are welcome here. Whether you are single and satisfied, single and dissatisfied, dating, engaged, married, partnered, separated, divorced, widowed, or in a (few) situationship(s), you are welcome here. Whether you have family or friends who love you and whom you love or whether you have had to or chose to do life on your own, you are welcome here. Each of us can benefit from heart awareness, heart integrity, and holistic heart health. I'm so glad you're giving it to yourself.

I.

YOUR RELATIONSHIP
WITH YOURSELF

ENHANCING SELF-COMPASSION

A s we begin this journey into the healing of our hearts, I invite
you to center in on enhancing, rebuilding, and nourishing
your self-compassion. Focus with a deep, soulful breath on shifting from neglecting yourself to honoring yourself. What does self-
compassion feel, look, sound, taste like for you? You may want to
journal your reflection on this question as a list, a poem, or even a
letter to yourself. As you shift from self-neglect, self-abandonment,
self-erasure, and/or self-hatred, you can authentically begin to
walk in the fullness of self-acceptance and self-respect.

To lay the groundwork, I want to start by asserting that your
growth is built on the idea that your love of yourself is *necessary*.
As you begin to think about the ways you may have been harsh
with, judgmental of, or shaming of yourself, weigh the cost. What
have been the consequences for you emotionally, physically, and
spiritually of demanding so much of yourself with minimal space
or time for soft landings?

On the other hand, what have you gained when you have lived
from a place of care? Imagine what would happen if you honored and respected yourself. What would happen if you treated
yourself in such a way that it became clear that your wellness and

wholeness are priorities? In this moment and in the chapters to come, I invite you to come home to yourself. Release that harsh way of thinking and treating yourself and learn to delight, enjoy, celebrate, and be at home with yourself. Yes?!

To be compassionate toward yourself means you have created space for the fullness of your complex identity and your complicated life, including your fractured heart. The aim is to be able to look at yourself with honesty and appreciation. Do you have appreciation, self-compassion, and respect for yourself? Even if the answer is yes (which is great!), do you recognize there is always room for growth?

In this chapter, I will cover a couple of key points that will help to enhance your self-compassion. The first is the significance of self-forgiveness. You may be upset with yourself and as a result be harsh with yourself, whether you are aware of it or not. Many of us are disappointed by the choices we have made and the ways our lives have turned out as a result of those choices—or even as a result of other people's choices that we had no control over. As a result, when you are angry, ashamed, and frustrated with yourself, you can rob yourself of any sense of peace. This self-judgment can lead to either giving up on yourself or being driven by intense perfectionism. Such perfectionism is based on the perpetual belief that you have so much to prove or to make up for that you cannot experience a sense of contentment or inner calm.

Think about the qualities or experiences that you constantly rehearse, recall, or reject about yourself. In which aspects of your life are you unable to give yourself a lot of grace or compassion when they come to mind?

When it comes to forgiveness, often we center our attention on other people, but I offer for your consideration that the healing of your heart may require that you forgive yourself. Offer forgiveness to yourself so that you can restore joy to your life or find joy for the first time, so you can reclaim or create for the first time a sense of peace. Self-forgiveness is a practice. It is an ongoing journey, an extended commitment. Each day is a new day, so even if you have forgiven yourself for some experiences of the past, when you think about today, yesterday, or this week, there may be new ones that you need let go of, or the old feelings may rise to the surface again. You may need to forgive yourself for the things you were hoping not to do. You may need to forgive yourself for the ways in which you participated in your failures or delays. You may need to forgive yourself for putting too much weight on yourself by setting unrealistic timelines or goals.

I invite you to say that you want to forgive yourself not just as a onetime event but as a choice to live your life in such a way that the grace and compassion you extend to others reach you as well.

You have given many chances to others while showing yourself so little grace, compassion, and forgiveness. It's time to shift the tide. Having self-compassion will begin to shift your one-sided relationships. Realizing you are worthy of change will free you from remaining in stagnant relationships.

Get free. Forgive yourself.

SELF-FORGIVENESS

You have given some people many chances because you love, respect, and care for them. You allow them a lot of leeway because you value being a loyal person even to disloyal people. That's your choice to make, and I have no authority or desire to tell you how many chances you should give someone. Instead, I would like you to contemplate loving, respecting, and caring about yourself enough, being loyal to yourself enough, to give *yourself* another chance, which includes forgiving yourself. This does not mean you will live without any sense of remorse or accountability, but it does mean you will not continue to view yourself and treat yourself based on the worst things you have done.

On occasion you have given people another chance because you are hopeful and optimistic that they can change. What about you? Do you believe that you can change—that you can shift your thinking, patterns, habits, or attitude? You have enough faith to believe others can. Believe that you are capable of it. What would shift right now, in this moment, if you let yourself change your perspective? Look at the story of your life again—not the moments you regret in harsh isolation, but the moments that led to the bad decisions, the unhealthy life patterns, the destructive tendencies. Look at yourself with eyes that see your past, present, and possible future. Breathe into the possibility of a new season. You do not have to forget your past, but you can choose to learn from it and transform your future. If this aligns with you, inhale through your nose. Exhale through your mouth. Release yourself, again and again.

Self-compassion requires not only self-forgiveness but also liberation from perfectionism. I open the door for you to walk into belief in your own evolution and growth. This is vital, because when you believe in false dichotomies—you are either a total success or a complete failure—then whenever you make a mistake, fall short, or live in a way that you were trying to break free from, you will start to think of yourself as a failure. You will create impossible standards for yourself and as a result think of yourself solely in the negative when really you're in a process of growth and change, as we all are. You are healing, transforming, climbing, and shifting. Yes!?! When you recognize you are in a developmental process that sometimes looks circular and always includes setbacks, you can be more understanding of and compassionate toward yourself, so that one mistake or setback—in fact, even several setbacks—does not have to define you or limit the ways in which you see your possibility.

As you think about your heart-healing journey, take note of the ways in which you are already changing. Perfection is not required. Simply take note of your growth. Appreciate and acknowledge yourself and your growth. Are you able to recognize the ways in which you have made positive shifts? Be mindful of the things that you can notice now that you would not have seen before. Soulfully take note of some ways you have advocated for yourself that you would have endured in silence in the past. Hold gratitude for yourself for the times that you have exited from or set boundaries in negative circumstances that you previously would have tolerated. I invite you to truly honor yourself for your beautiful growth—not perfection but growth.

Shifting from your self-critical voice to your self-compassionate voice means that you can see and hold yourself gently. I hope that as your heart-healing journey starts, you can recognize the progress you have already made in your relationships with yourself and others.

Intentionally give yourself permission to look for your progress. You will begin to see what you're looking for, and this new insight will increase your self-compassion. Enhance this progress by looking back on your journal entries or social media posts. See what has captured your mind and how you have responded to the events and people around you, as well as the dynamics occurring within you. If you are in therapy, let your therapist know that you want to spend some time reflecting on your growth from when you started working with that person to where you are now. It is a beautiful experience when those who are in your life acknowledge the positive changes that they themselves have observed as well. And while a therapist, family member, friends, or coworkers can notice the change, you must also be able to see it within yourself. You will enhance your self-compassion when you set the intention of looking for your growth. When you become intentional about looking for your progress, you will more readily learn to recognize it instead of always focusing on your mistakes or shortcomings.

GRATITUDE

Another way to build self-compassion is by becoming intentionally grateful to yourself for the steps you have taken to honor and care for yourself and your dreams. In a video that went viral, rapper Snoop Dogg was receiving his star on the Hollywood Walk of Fame. He says, "I want to thank me for believing in me." People found his comment humorous, as we are used to thanking God, others, and even corporations, but it is rare to hear someone express appreciation to themselves for having invested the time, energy, and talent into manifesting their dreams. While it might feel awkward or even make you chuckle, consider what are you are grateful to yourself for—perhaps deciding to continue your healing journey, or leaving work on time today so you could relax, or decluttering your space, or reaching out to an old or a new friend. Engaging in practices of self-care are loving, compassionate acts that are foundational to a heartful life.

We often remember to thank other people. Hopefully you thank people when they extend kindness to you. I wonder if you are able to have gratitude for yourself: for your body, heart, mind, and spirit that have been with you on this journey. Your nervous system has been working overtime to protect you, to keep you safe, to try to keep you grounded and regulated. Your mind has been working all day, every day trying to figure everything out, to find solutions, to look for the path forward, to make sense of the chaos, to transform your life. And at this very moment, your body is working hard; your senses, organs, muscles, and heart are all engaged in a complex choreography for you to live from one moment to the next. Do you consider the orchestra that is playing within you each second for you to live, breathe, and move?

You are here not only in body, heart, and mind, but also in soul. Your soul has been doing so much for your survival and your flourishing. With all of that happening within you, I invite you to really enter a state of gratitude and appreciation for the steps you have taken toward healing.

You can find gratitude for what you have done and also gratitude for what is going well in your life. We often focus on things that are not what we want them to be, but it is my hope that as you look around at the landscape of your life, there are some things that you have appreciation for. You have really worked hard psychologically and/or practically to nourish some seeds that have sprouted and grown. That gratitude and recognition of your effort will guide you toward more self-compassion. We often attend to the crops that failed, but please give attention to the fruits of your labor that have shown results. You may have been intentional and created better relationships or adopted healthier habits or changed the way you handle your finances. Appreciate yourself.

STOP OVEREXTENDING

Another way to enhance your self-compassion is by monitoring your generosity. Overextending yourself can result in depletion, which is counter to self-compassion. It is beautiful to be a generous person. From a morals and values place, generosity improves the lives of others and can also benefit you, as it allows you to be a blessing to others, create meaning, and have an impact. At the same time, when you dishonor, disrespect, or abandon yourself, you can create a lifestyle of overextending yourself that drains you, dishonors your humanity, and has a bad effect on your health and wellness. You may need to set more boundaries, give yourself permission to say no, learn when to exit spaces and situations, and recognize when you are being disrespected, used, or dishonored. To build self-compassion, learn to use your discernment and voice. What have you agreed to do that has resulted in your being exhausted, overextended, and perhaps even resentful? Use your agency, your power to choose. To choose your wellness you will need to learn the holiness of no. What are your sleep and eating habits, work hours, eyes, and heart telling you about being overextended?

It is self-compassion to choose your care and resist the idea that self-care is selfish. I invite you to say this aloud: "I am deserving of care. I am deserving of rest. I am deserving of love. I am worthy. I am enough. I can say yes to myself. I choose my wellness. My body is a temple and I come home to it with compassion."

When you are making decisions, consider the consequences of them on your mental health. Make choices that reflect your priority to live well: joyfully, healthily, mindfully, and soulfully. If these are your priorities and values, they need to manifest in some action, in some behaviors. If you want to heal your heart, show some sign that this is your intention. Readjust your schedule, habits, patterns, and boundaries. To honor yourself and to be compassionate toward yourself, what calls do you no longer need to make or accept? Where do you no longer need to go? What are the habits of overextension that you want to be intentional about releasing and replacing? What are the ways of working and of resting that you want to shift so that you can better protect and preserve yourself? You are worthy of these changes. You are entitled to protect your time, peace, and health.

FOSTERING SELF-UNDERSTANDING

To cultivate self-compassion is to choose self-understanding over self-judgment. Look at the various chapters of your life and seek to understand how you landed there. Now take a deeper look instead of dismissing your journey with thoughts such as *What's wrong with me?* or *How could I be so stupid?* or *I'm so weak.* The labels that we give ourselves or that other people have given us keep us stuck. Let me be clear, I am not talking about making excuses, which can also keep us stuck. You should accept responsibility when you mess up. Instead, I am talking about understanding yourself more fully so you can be empowered to go forward toward your healing. When you understand, with grace, how and why you made earlier choices, you experience the liberation to make different ones the next time around. When you don't understand yourself, you will look back at your acts harshly, even with hostility, ridicule, or intense shame, so instead try to consider (1) What was I thinking, and where did the thoughts that led to that behavior come from? (2) What is the source of my decision? That is to say, what in my life's journey shaped me in such a way that I ended up choosing this way of thinking, choosing, or acting? When you understand the root of those behaviors or events, this doesn't mean that you are going to give up because you can't change the past. No! Instead, you realize with grace and compassion that this is what led you here *and* you don't have to continue choosing this mindset or behavior. You can be empowered to make a new choice. You care enough about yourself that you don't give the pain or dysfunction of your past the final say.

Give yourself permission to break out of those cycles and patterns and to learn something new. You can be compassionate with yourself even as you are learning, knowing that you are worthy of new possibilities.

Sabrina is a married new mother who landed her dream job a few months ago. It is a promotion in title and income and exceeds the goals she has set for herself. Her hard work has paid off, and she is excited to stretch her leadership skills. The challenges are the commute and the supervisor. The commute is ninety minutes each way in traffic. Although Sabrina is supposed to be the director of the center, the person who has oversight for the region doesn't want her to make any changes and is fostering dissent among those who report to her. After wrestling with her decision and discussing it with her family and in therapy, Sabrina takes the courageous step of looking for and accepting another job. She decides her mental health and family time are more important than the title and status. The new position is closer to her home, and the new workplace environment is more supportive. In the past, Sabrina would have stayed and felt she had to win everyone over to prove her own worth. In this season of her life, she is celebrating her new priority: her own heart.

As you heal and grow, I invite you to breathe life into your possibility and to breathe with grace and compassion into your present moment. As poet Joel Cross reminds us, you can be the love of your life. Many of us love deeply, and out of the depths of our love, we give to others and do some incredible things. Love can lead you to some courageous, bodacious, unconventional acts. What would it look like for you to love yourself that boldly? What edifying gesture of self-compassion will you commit to doing for yourself, not rarely but regularly? In your self-compassionate care of yourself, can you be as committed, faithful, and loyal to the care of your own soul, body, mind, and heart as you have been to the care of others? Self-compassion can literally shift the trajectory of your life. You are deserving of the shift.

ACTIVATION EXERCISE: Write a love letter to yourself. Make it full of appreciation, understanding, forgiveness, and self-preservation.

AFFIRMATION: If it aligns with you, place both hands on your heart and speak aloud the words "My heart is healing, and so it is."

2

HEALING SELF-ABANDONMENT, SELF-NEGLECT, AND PEOPLE-PLEASING

Charisma is a Christian Black woman in her early thirties. Throughout her life she has been given the message that a good woman, a good Black woman, and especially a good Christian Black woman sacrifices herself for the well-being of others. This message was given to her directly and indirectly from her family, friends, dating partners, church, television shows, music lyrics, celebrity role models, and social media. The messages included such themes as "Thinking about yourself is selfish, and you don't want to be selfish." And "A career-minded woman will never be a good spouse or mother, so focus on making your spouse's dreams and your children's dreams come true—not your own." And "God wants you to forget about yourself and focus on God and people who need you." And "The only way the Black community and especially Black men will survive is if Black women prioritize the community and the healing of Black men." And finally "Black women who are upset, disappointed, sad, or angry are unlovable, so never have a bad attitude no matter what heartache you are facing." Charisma did not consciously believe these notions were true, but unconsciously they drove her to abandon herself and perpetually seek to please

others, even if that required dishonoring herself. Charisma
needs to attend to matters of the heart.

What is your story? Beloved, what or who taught you that you had to abandon or neglect yourself in order to be a good or lovable person? Was it messages about your race, gender, religion, sexuality, disability, age? What did you see or hear that caused you to believe the path to good loving required that you surrender yourself along the way?

To heal self-abandonment and self-neglect, you have to first recognize the ways it shows up in your life. Let me first say that self-abandonment and self-neglect are not just about your behavior but also the frequency of it. The issue is not just that you put the needs of others ahead of your own but also that this is a perpetual way of being in the world. It's one thing if you stay up late one night doing something for someone else, but when it becomes a pattern, you have abandoned yourself.

Self-abandonment or self-erasure are when you are so focused on those around you that you lose sight of your interior—the truth of yourself. Foundational to healthy relationships is to see and hear your heart speak. Let your heart sing your true song instead of someone else's or everyone else's.

So how do we abandon ourselves?

You may have erased yourself in pursuit of others. You may have been so focused on being who others wanted you to be that you never paid attention to who you truly are. Has it been so crucial for you to get the approval of your parents, of a potential partner, or of a mentor or supervisor that you neglected the desires of your heart? Do you make your educational, work, romantic, financial, and even spiritual choices based on the script handed to you, even when everything within you is screaming that this is not you? You do not have to forsake yourself. Can you imagine that as a possibility? Yes, culture, family, and tradition can be significant. Your soul is important as well. Is there room for you at the table of all those who influence you? Is social media dictating your life: your fashion, food, relationships? To show up with your heart, you can no longer mindlessly follow other people, trends, and the media. Instead you can move from clarity grounded in truth and centered around authenticity. Instead of being a leaf blowing in the wind, seeking money, popularity, and external validation, you can set your compass and walk always in truth.

You may be abandoning yourself through people-pleasing. You may occasionally or often forget your values because of your focus on other people's values and priorities. To relate to people who don't hold your values, are you engaging in incongruent actions at work or in your dating life? You may be hoping to be chosen, selected, or deemed worthy, and as a result you have adopted or pretended to adopt the speech, values, and tendencies of others.

Abandoning yourself can also look like hiding parts of yourself—your feelings, thoughts, and priorities. Be honest with yourself about the ways and times you have diluted and disguised yourself to be acceptable to others. If you are perpetually censoring yourself in your interactions with others, not even telling yourself the truth, it can cost you your freedom.

Another form of self-abandonment is not trusting yourself. It's time to stop ignoring the voice within you—your inner spirit, your intuition. You can no longer afford to second-guess yourself. When you perpetually ask others to make your decisions, you have falsely concluded that everyone else must know better than you. You may doubt yourself because of mistakes you have made in the past, acts of betrayal by someone you opened up to, or traumatic events. In mujerista psychology, which is the psychology developed by and for Latinas, Dr. Lillian Comas-Díaz encourages us to reclaim and reconnect with our intuition as an act of resistance and healing. It is vital to begin trusting yourself.

Self-abandonment is evident when you are self-critical, condemning, judgmental, harsh, and unable to celebrate your accomplishments. The constant self-criticism wears you down. It may even cause you to neglect your self-care. You may focus on work and others and ignore your own body's needs for rest and nourishment. Consider how you may have neglected yourself spiritually, emotionally, and financially this month. Fixing financial self-abandonment means considering the ways you approach your resources that may set you up for more stress or engagement with people who don't care about you. (Financial self-abandonment is not the same as poverty, classism, and exploitation by other individuals and systems. These factors need to be addressed as systemic barriers and inequities.)

Finally, you may abandon yourself by silencing yourself, not speaking up for yourself. Perhaps you are protecting the feelings and wants of others and sacrificing your peace, health, safety, and well-being. If you are not a trauma survivor, you may wonder why you are engaging in these behaviors at all. Perhaps you grew up being the emotional caretaker for your parents or siblings. Did you learn to silence yourself and always put others first? While it is a beautiful intention to be loving, generous, and caring, I invite you to recognize that the nourishing of your own heart is beautiful as well. As you tend to your heart, you may want to make a decision to no longer collude with those who are disrespecting, demeaning, and dishonoring you. You can commit in this moment that you will not participate in the false dichotomy or false choice that says to be a loving person you must neglect yourself. Learn to let that love flow inward and outward.

Tony is a single thirtysomething two-spirit indigenous person. He is the eldest sibling and has a lot of family responsibilities. Tony feels honored to be able to help his family and enjoys their admiration. At the same time, the long hours Tony works at two jobs, the meals skipped, and the lack of sleep are taking a toll. Tony has migraines and has become increasingly irritable with his younger siblings, often yelling at them for little things. As a result, they have begun to shun Tony, which is even more upsetting, as he provides for them financially and emotionally. Tony needs to find ways to enhance his self-love and nourishment even while continuing to show his family love.

Consider what self-abandonment, neglect, erasure, and people-pleasing have cost you—perhaps peace, health, self-expression, joy, love, and years of your life. It's time that you tend to the garden of your heart even as you value the gardens of others.

Hopefully by now you can recognize some ways you may have abandoned yourself in the past or present and can be honest with yourself about those costs. The question remains: *How do I heal and shift?* I'm glad you asked.

1. Learn to trust yourself. Perhaps you have developed the habit of always letting other people make decisions for you. It's time to start trusting yourself. This shift cannot just be mental. You have to change your behaviors. Begin to actively take part in your decision-making. Of course you can still consult your wisdom circle—people whose opinions you value—but you also want to become a person whose opinion you value. Practice reflecting, weighing different outcomes, considering the potential benefits and costs, and seeing what your heart, mind,

and spirit are saying. Do not keep suppressing your voice. There is wisdom within you.

2. Check in with yourself. You may not be used to tuning in to yourself. There are pathways that can help you discover what your heart is saying.

   • Take undistracted time in silence to reflect. In other words, set aside time without social media, television, or other people's voices, and seek your authentic truth in silence. Some people like to take this time when they're bathing, driving, or walking. Others prefer to meditate or simply sit in stillness. Experiment to see what you prefer.

   • Seek your voice through journaling. Set aside time to journal at the start or the end of your day. You can journal based on a prompt or a specific idea, problem, or goal, or you can journal in free form, with openness to writing about whatever issues come to you in the moment.

   • Explore your heart through the arts. Writing or reading poetry, listening to music, singing, dancing, and experiencing or creating visual art are great forms of self-expression that psychologists have found can enhance self-awareness.

   • Delve into spiritual practices. When you are praying, reading sacred texts, meditating, or listening to spiritual and religious teachers, notice what comes up related to the matters of your heart.

   • Pay attention to your body. When you are in certain places, with certain people, or engaged in particular activities, notice what is happening in your body. You heart may race with enthusiasm or with anxiety. You may feel bored and uninterested or awakened and energized. You may have a knot in your stomach or a sinking, heavy feeling of pressure. Notice and give yourself permission to be honest about what you feel, whether it is joy or regret. Pay attention. That is your heart speaking.

3. Set boundaries. As you decide not to abandon yourself, you will note some ripple effects. To choose yourself, what obligations and relationships do you need to release? To attend to your heart and live from a place of truth, you may need to let go of some people and activities that are no longer aligned with your wholeness and wellness; in truth, perhaps they never were. The good news is that while you may need to say some goodbyes, you also get to create space for hellos. Your boundaries carve out space in your life for fullhearted yeses. You are deserving of some passionate yeses—not just hesitant, duty-bound yeses. It's time.

4. Give yourself permission to be different. To shift from people-pleasing, you will need to become okay with rejection. When you show up as yourself and for yourself, some people will not like you. There are people who only want a clone, a puppet, someone who will always agree with them and do what they want. You can be at peace with others not liking you, because you value living authentically more highly. This transition will be awkward but liberating. You don't have to be a puppet, perpetually altering yourself based on others' facial expressions, comments, and actions. I hope you can be free and committed to truth even when it comes with some rejection. I'm

not talking about becoming rude, selfish, or inconsiderate. I'm talking about living with more honesty, because while you value relationships, you also value singing your own song instead of lip-synching everyone else's.

5. Be gentle with yourself. Release any harshness. Being self-critical leaves you little room to care for yourself. I invite you to consider what it will look, sound, and feel like for you to soften. Try a little tenderness. When you are tender with yourself, when you handle yourself thoughtfully, you will be less likely to erase yourself. That voice within—your heart, body, and spirit—may be saying to you in this moment: "Don't discard me again. Don't leave me behind. Love me and care for me. I'm tired. Let me rest. Choose restoration for me. I need you to choose me." Deem yourself worthy of your own care and consideration. You may often think and speak of others mistreating you. What are the ways you have not been caring for yourself? Choose yourself again or for the first time. See yourself through the eyes of tenderness.

This may be the perfect time for you to take a cleansing breath. And another one.

You can grieve the trauma, abandonment, stress, grief, and disappointment that led you on this path of people-pleasing, self-neglect, and self-abandonment. Recognize the grief and then acknowledge that you can make a different choice. Embrace this new opportunity to live from truth and tenderness. Learn to love others without leaving yourself behind.

Wherever you are going, take yourself with you. Don't abandon yourself. Go back and get yourself. Seize your voice, time, interests, and truth. In this season, you want to claim your wellness and peace. You can choose to live in truth. Embrace the ways you are unique. Your soul has a particular imprint, and that's a good thing. Decide to shift from self-neglect to self-love as you commit to no longer abandoning yourself.

Roger, who grew up impoverished, is a driven workaholic. He never makes time to work out or socialize, because he fears that if he relaxes, he will end up destitute. He is startled by his recent medical results. Within just two years, his health has declined, and medical tests show that he has high blood pressure and is at risk for diabetes. The fact that he had a beloved grandmother who died from diabetes-related complications makes these results especially alarming. Roger makes drastic changes in his habits and is able to maintain them for the last few years. He adopts a better diet, creates a regular exercise routine, and is even dating someone he met at a cooking class. Roger is still successful, but instead of giving all of himself to his work, he is engaged in a more nourishing, holistic life.

ACTIVATION EXERCISE: Write a vow of one activity you will do at least once a week to nourish yourself. It may be physical, emotional, spiritual, social, or financial. Choose self-care over self-abandonment. You can show up more enriched in your relationships when you have taken care of yourself. And whether you have close relationships or not, self-care is essential.

AFFIRMATION: If it aligns with you, place one hand on your forehead and declare, "I will not neglect myself. I can love others while still loving myself. I reclaim me."

3

HEALING INSECURITY AND UNWORTHINESS

Karissa is a neurodivergent woman in her late thirties. She is unhappily married and feels stuck. She isn't comfortable speaking up to her husband about the things he does that she doesn't like, because she doesn't want to be seen as "one of those women" who complains a lot. While Karissa was growing up, her mother suffered in silence and maintained that nags run their husbands away. In a confirmation of this viewpoint, Karissa's husband frequently praises her to his friends because she doesn't nag him or give him a hard time like their wives do. She also doesn't want to leave the marriage because she was not popular on the dating scene and fears if she leaves her husband, she will end up alone. Karissa's insecurities have her locked in a very hard place.

Derrick is a single man in his forties who lives with his mother. He has a good job but no friends. Growing up, he was teased about his appearance. He approached one girl in high school and two in college. None of them were interested. As the years passed, he became more anxious about possible rejection and has not asked anyone else out. He does his socializing on dating *apps, social media where he doesn't have any pictures up, and porn sites. He enjoys talking to women in these places for a few days but then stops interacting once they express an interest in meeting in person, because he fears they will find him unattractive and reject him. Derrick's fear of being unworthy of love has him locked in a self-fulfilling prophecy where he blocks any potential love from showing up in his life.*

Visualize yourself laying down the weights of insecurity and unworthiness that have blocked your love life. See yourself dancing free with your heart open. Imagine yourself standing in the truth that you are worthy of love from yourself and others.

Acknowledge where the insecurity and sense of unworthiness came from. Often it emerged from early critical voices that shamed you. They told you that you were not smart enough, cute enough, talented enough, or good enough. The voices may have been peers, relatives, teachers, or even strangers. That critical voice within didn't start with you. As you got older, you may have experienced being rejected or mistreated at school, at work, or in social settings. Some people decided you were trying to be too much and that you could not have the life of your dreams. Now even if you're not in their presence, you say those negative things to yourself about your looks, intelligence, and worthiness.

There are different domains of self-esteem. You may feel good about yourself intellectually but feel insecure about your appearance. You may feel good about certain talents and abilities but feel insecure socially. Some of us are quick to say that we love ourselves, but when it comes to relationships and love, we have a lot of self-doubt and insecurity. You may question if you are worthy of love, because you have never experienced it. It's essential to build your confidence and ability to celebrate and validate yourself so you don't go into the world desperate for affirmation. You may be hungry for love but then can't receive it, or you may not believe any attention or compliments you receive are sincere.

You need to be at home being yourself. Be confident enough to show up as yourself, knowing that the right people will appreciate you, and those who don't are not meant for you. Being authentic lays the groundwork for clarity about relationships that align and those that don't. Start by liking and loving yourself. Notice the qualities that you appreciate instead of constantly putting yourself down. When self-criticism is your soundtrack, you will sabotage the possibility that love will flow in your direction.

Instead of shrinking into the background or pretending to be something you're not, focus on being freely yourself. Who are you when you are not trying to impress, seduce, or persuade others? Healing insecurity requires resting within the peace and truth of who you are. Yes, it can be scary to risk being yourself knowing that some people will reject you, but the first person who needs to choose you is you. Choose yourself and then let everything flow from there.

RELEASE COMPARISON

Mia is a bisexual Latina graduate student. When she and her partner are at home alone, she feels comfortable in the relationship. When they go out with other couples, she finds herself constantly comparing her partner to others and ends up questioning her love and investment in the relationship. By the time they get home, she has worked herself up and is anxious, afraid, and annoyed. She noticed that one person's partner had their arm around them the whole time and wonders why her partner didn't do that. She noticed that one person gave their partner lots of compliments and wants to know why her partner didn't do that. She noticed one couple giggled a lot while exchanging intimate looks and private jokes. She is disappointed that she and her partner didn't do that.

Insecurity can have you not only constantly comparing yourself to other people but also comparing your relationships to those of others. For your security and worthiness, consider that people from all walks of life can be lovable or worthy of love. When you approach love from the vantage point of scarcity, you may believe that only people with a specific height, weight, income, hair type, color of eyes, accent, or education are lovable. This is absolutely not true. Instead of believing that someone else's existence disqualifies you from love, shift into knowing that both of you are worthy.

Don't make other people your thermometer, either. Instead, pay attention to the voice within you that will let you know how you feel in this relationship or friendship. If another couple does something you don't do, you can be happy for them either while cultivating similar behavior in your own relationship or without feeling the need to duplicate their actions.

SHIFT YOUR FOCUS

Insecurity is fed by focusing on your weaknesses, mistakes, and lowest moments. Consider which aspects of your life you focus your time and energy on. When we are depressed, despairing, or insecure, our minds tend to home in on the negative. This creates a kind of self-fulfilling prophecy, a tale you are telling yourself about yourself. You are worthy of a new story. For love to flow to yourself and others, you need a story that affirms your worthiness for love.

I invite you to consider the things you appreciate about yourself: your strengths, your positive qualities, your growth areas. Reflect on times you have been loving, kind, thoughtful, and caring. Insecurity makes you highlight your shortcomings and ignore your strengths. Stop overgeneralizing. There is more to you than your mistakes. Start telling yourself the full truth. Forgive and free yourself so you can be your own friend, be your own beloved. Security comes in part from a grounding in self-love. You are not waiting for someone to give you the security of their validation. Let others encounter you as someone who really likes and loves themselves—not in an egotistical way but in the way that shows you have watered your own garden. You are not dehydrated, holding a hose but waiting for someone else to give you water.

Then when you do consider your weaknesses or mistakes, you can look at them with honesty, humility, and wisdom from the lessons learned. Growth in matters of the heart requires recognizing that love for yourself does not require you to be perfect. You can love yourself in your present condition. This would be a beautiful moment to take a cleansing breath. Perfection is not required for you to love yourself. Yes?!

Jasmine is a single woman. She terminated a pregnancy in college and has felt guilty and ashamed of this for years. She believes God is angry with her, and she is angry at herself. She rarely creates any space in her life for breath, lightness, ease, or laughter. She would be considered by most to be a driven, ambitious workaholic. She works out for two hours a day and lives a disciplined life. Her only outlet for joy is volunteerism. She loves giving to others and does that regularly through a meal program at her church. Jasmine falsely believes she is unworthy of receiving the love she expresses weekly to the unhoused community in her city.

You may be holding yourself hostage based on experiences in your past. It may be related to something you have done or something others have done to you or said about you. Scripture teaches that nothing can separate us from God's love (see Romans 8:31–39). Whether you believe in God or not, I invite you to consider what you think has permanently separated you or disqualified you from love. To embrace self-love, you will need to release yourself, stop punishing yourself, and give yourself permission to let love flow to you and from you.

What do you think disqualifies you from love? Challenge the lie of your unworthiness. Do you blame your appearance, income, mental illness, or past unhealthy relationships? What would shift in you and around you if you believed you are worthy of love, as we all are? You are not beyond the reach of love. It all starts with love of yourself and love of the Creator, whatever that means to you. Sacred love and self-love will build your confidence. Consider what you're good at: who you are, what you can do, what you bring to relationships. You very likely take your strong points for granted. You also may ignore the effort you have made to build up certain skills. Learn to be confident enough to fail. You don't have to get everything right. Give yourself the grace and freedom to try. Love is worth the risk. You are worth the risk. Authentic love for yourself can guide you, and when it's balanced by truth, you will not operate in ego and arrogance. Grounded love, love with humility, is healthy whether you are in or out of intimate relationships.

Bentu is a woman in her sixties. She married someone much older than she was and felt more like a caretaker than a spouse. Her husband, who was often cruel the older and sicker he became, died ten years ago. The marriage was not a happy one, and now she feels she made the wrong choices and missed her chance at love. She spends all of her time giving to family and community members. She is loved by many, but she still feels lonely and disappointed that she has never enjoyed true romantic love.

Whatever your age, I want you to know that love is still possible. Can you allow yourself to consider that perhaps you didn't miss it? You're not too late. Love is not just for those in their twenties and thirties. Love is not just for those who are entering their first marriage. With all the detours and disappointments, love can still be your destination. Trust this present moment. Show up for yourself with love. You are a fount of wisdom and lessons learned, and you still have so much to give *and* so much you have never received.

Another approach to addressing insecurity is to examine your cognitive distortions. What are the lies that drive your insecurity and sense of unworthiness? Look at the evidence for and against these beliefs so that you can dismantle them. You may believe you're not worthy of love because people "never" show up for you in love. The truth may be that a lot of people let you down, yet surely there was at least one person who showed you loving care that was genuine, no matter how brief it was. Perhaps it was a teacher, a neighbor, a childhood friend, a coworker, or a stranger. You may believe you're unworthy because of the ways you have been mistreated. I want you to know that when people dishonor or disrespect you, it is reflective of their state of mind, not yours. You are worthy of love even if you have never been made to feel like it. If your feelings of unworthiness are rooted in oppression, please know that oppressive people lie. Marginalized people are judged unworthy to justify the mistreatment of them. So if you have been made to feel that you are not enough because of colorism, racism, sexism, classism, ableism, heterosexism, or xenophobia, know that these are intentional lies. You are lovely, lovable, and worthy of love, including self-love.

Finally, I invite you to affirm that you will not let insecurity sabotage your relationships. What does this mean? It means you don't have to be reactive, defensive, or combative. You also don't have to contort yourself, beg, plead, or convince someone that you are worthy of love. You can be settled within yourself and from that grounded place receive those who are for you and release those who do not value, appreciate, or love you.

Amanda was a straight-A student throughout school and an incredible soccer player. She was always praised for her grades and athleticism. She had lots of friends from her sports teams and neighborhood but had never had a romantic relationship. At first she dismissed this as being due to her height. She was always taller than most of the boys and had been told by family and friends that she just had to wait for the boys to grow to catch up with her. She went to college with great expectations for an exciting dating life. As she moved from college graduation and through her twenties without being asked out, she began to wonder if there was some issue besides her height. As she moved into her thirties with still not one date, she resigned herself to the belief that she was not worthy of love. In therapy, we begin to open up her imagination, to reawaken her hope. We explore how she might show up in the world differently if she believed that she was worthy of romance, care, interest, and even a loving relationship. A few months after Amanda sets this intention, a coworker asks her out for lunch. After they have been dating a few weeks, he jokingly shares that she was always super serious and seemed to have a wall up, so he had to work up the confidence to ask her out. She acknowledges jokingly to me that from all the messages she had been given, she had unconsciously assumed that any man she dates has to be taller than her. She realizes that she had never considered men that are her height or shorter as potential partners. She assumed that they wouldn't be interested. Her new special friend is her height when she's not wearing heels, she tells me, and she is having the time of her life.

ACTIVATION EXERCISE: Complete the following sentences three times.

1. I release the lie that_____.
   I affirm that _____.

2. I release the lie that _____.
   I affirm that _____.

3. I release the lie that _____.
   I affirm that _____.

ACTIVATION EXERCISE: Complete this poem by filling in the blanks.

My heart is healing, growing, and _____.

I attract love into my life with my _____.

I pour love into those I care about with _____.

_____ sings my worthiness.

_____whispers my worthiness.

I shift from frantic to _____ as I

securely embrace my _____.

AFFIRMATION: If it aligns with you, embrace yourself and read your poem aloud either to yourself or to someone you feel comfortable sharing it with.

II.

FOUNDATIONS
OF HEALTHY RELATIONSHIPS

4

BUILDING HEALTHY FRIENDSHIPS AND ROMANTIC RELATIONSHIPS

Natalie is a Haitian American single woman in her twenties. Her family has faced intergenerational trauma, including migration stress, which has made trust and emotional connection difficult. They spend a lot of time together, but many topics are considered unmentionable. She loves her family and also has a great group of friends, both at work and outside of work. She would like to better understand her patterns and how they may have affected the way she showed up in the few romantic relationships she has had. She is hoping to have a healthy marriage and to become a mother someday.

Chin is a married Chinese American man with two children. He's been feeling depressed about some financial losses in his business. He has tried to handle things on his own, as he feels it's his responsibility to take care of his family. He recently overheard his wife on the phone talking about him and was disappointed to learn that she is not happy because she knows something is wrong but doesn't know what. Chin is trying to figure out what it means to be a good husband and how to feel better about himself.

Whether you come from a loving family or not, whether you have a lot of experience dating or not, and whether you have a loving friendship circle or not, you can build healthy or healthier friendships and romantic relationships. In this chapter, I will share with you five foundational priorities for building healthy relationships.

BUILDING BLOCK 1.
SELF-LOVE AND SELF-CARE

The first section of this book covered this foundational truth, because if you don't love yourself, you are more likely to experience detrimental dynamics in your relationships. A lack of self-love can cause you to choose or remain in unhealthy relationships. This lack of self-love can also cause you to doubt and reject love because you don't feel worthy of it. Finally, a lack of self-love can cause you to diminish yourself in the hopes of attracting or keeping a friend or romantic partner. When it comes to family relationships, you may falsely believe that to love and honor your relatives, you have to be willing to diminish or dishonor yourself.

Your self-love will motivate your self-care. You are healthier in relationships when you are taking care of yourself. While it is true that good friendships and relationships can enhance our health, physically and emotionally, we also play a role in our own wholeness. Imagine if you stay up late every night, skip meals or live off fast food and caffeine, abuse substances, and have trouble setting boundaries, resulting in your taking work home with you and perpetually saying yes to requests from people that leave you drained. How do you imagine you will show up when it comes time to spend the evening with your partner or friend? You will likely be tired, sapped of energy, annoyed, irritated, resentful, and overwhelmed. Creating some ease in your life with self-care will also make you a soft landing place for your loved ones. Of course, there are times when crises arise and sacrifices must made, but consider if you are constantly living your life in crisis, neglecting yourself in the process. It may be time to make a change. When we are not in a good place, we may become destructive or controlling. Contemplate the things you are already doing for your wellness—like reading this book. Allow yourself to think of other ways you can express your care and love for yourself. Getting exercise, going to therapy, or starting your day with a spiritual practice such as prayer or meditation may allow you to have more space in your heart for breath, love, joy, and peace. A loving friend or partner can show up for the co-labor of building a healthy relationship. You and your loved ones deserve that version of you. As you love yourself, you can show up more grounded, honest, and clear. These are foundational elements to good loving.

BUILDING BLOCK 2. LOVE

For a healthy relationship to survive, thrive, and flourish, love is vital. Love is not just a feeling. Love is a decision and a verb. It guides your feelings, thoughts, and behaviors. Love will have you show up for someone even when you're tired. Love will give someone the benefit of the doubt instead of always expecting the worst. Love gives understanding, acceptance, and support. You can love someone in the different seasons of your life and the different seasons of their life. Love is sacred and holistic. You can love someone physically, emotionally, spiritually, and behaviorally. There is fruit or evidence of love. It cannot be hidden. It will reveal itself in your words and actions. It shows itself in your facial expressions and body language. It feeds and nourishes itself. Love births greater and deeper love. It involves not just lust for the physical—typical of the honeymoon phase of initial passion—but also true enjoyment of the other. Authentic love persists over time. Love connects you so that you grieve with your loved one and celebrate with them as well. Love makes you thoughtful and concerned about the well-being of the other. Love lifts. It does not seek to destroy, break, or control. Love expands you to your fullest state. It does not require that you shrink yourself. I invite you to think about the fruit of your love. Consider the ways you express your love in words, romantic behavior, and everyday acts of kindness and service. It's time to break out of any scripts that have told you that you are not a loving person. You can decide to be more loving today. I think by reading this book, you are already moving in the direction of love.

BUILDING BLOCK 3.
REALISTIC EXPECTATIONS

Hopefully you have a sense of the qualities you would like in a friend or partner, and you should consider these qualities for yourself as well. In other words, if you want someone who is trustworthy, spiritually minded, and generous, are these qualities you are also developing in yourself? When it comes to traits you would like in another, whether you consider these expectations or standards, reflect on which are optional and which are essential. You may want someone who would like to travel with you. Is a love of travel necessary or preferred? You may value spending a lot of time together, but is that preferred or necessary? These are important questions to ask because it will determine if you can happily be the partner of someone who works long hours or who travels for work. Likewise in friendship, if someone doesn't call you once a week to check in, would you consider them not a good friend? When we put expectations on people, we aren't necessarily desiring too much, but we may want it from the wrong person.

The things you want may not align with the skill set or personality of the person you are choosing.

> *Deborah and Jack are an African American couple in their fifties who married during their late twenties. They have children and grandchildren. She likes foreign films, while he likes action movies. She likes reading and listening to music, and he likes watching television. They love each other and are happy in their marriage. They sometimes engage in the entertainment choice that the other prefers and they sometimes do their own thing. The consistent truth is that they don't consider those activities the essence of who they are. They choose each other above all else, and both of them feel valued, loved, and appreciated. They also learned long ago to let some things go. Deborah was a literature major in college and would love to receive long love letters and poems. Jack is, as he would put it, "not a word guy," so he gives occasional flowers and the card is simply signed "Love, Jack." Jack loves to spend time with his family of origin. Early in their marriage, some things were said that made Deborah feel unwelcomed by his family members. The solution Deborah and Jack have worked out is that sometimes she goes with him to visit his family; sometimes if she decides not to go, he visits without her; and sometimes he skips a family gathering to stay home with her. Good times and challenging times, they continue showing up for each other in love.*

To build a healthy relationship, consider what you want and whether the person you are with is capable of and willing to give you these things. We have to be careful because sometimes we fall in love with a person's potential or our idea of who we would like them to be. Instead of trying to make them in your image and likeness, ask yourself if you can accept and appreciate them for who they are. Some people are unwilling to or incapable of being what you want them to be. It is unhealthy to keep expecting people to be who they're not or to constantly try to change someone who doesn't want to change. If you want them to be someone else, perhaps you don't actually love or even like them. You want to choose the truth of this person and to be chosen for your truth. Of course we all change and grow and hopefully become better together, but sometimes we are trying to transform someone into a person that they don't want to be or don't have the capacity to be.

This is true in friendships and family relationships as well. You can set yourself up for disappointment and the other person up for frustration if you keep wanting them to be something they are not. Perhaps your friend doesn't remember all the dates of events in your life; you can decide to give that person reminders, or you can decide this is not the kind of friend you need and release them. Your aunt may never give compliments, even if you ask her if she likes something about you, so you have to decide if you want to accept and enjoy her for what she does offer you as her expression of love, or you can decide you're not going to keep spending your weekends with her. What are you expecting or wanting, and who are you wanting it from? Does your desire line up with the truth of this person, and if not, do you want to accept them as they are or change the nature of the relationship?

Hold on to clarity about who people are. People can sense if you accept, reject, or merely tolerate them. None of us like to feel unacceptable to someone we consider a friend, relative, or romantic partner. This doesn't mean you should not share things you would prefer—but then you have to be prepared for their answer, in words and actions. You need to consider if you are willing to adjust your expectations, accept the person and their behavior, or shift your ideas about what the friendship or relationship will be. Deep intimacy and connection are built on acceptance of who we are at the core. A liberated love, whether platonic friendship or romantic relationship, is established in knowing and appreciating another for who they are and who we are when we're together.

There are things you desire in a connection that some people will make you feel are burdensome or too much, while others would do those things without you even having to ask. Some people will be annoyed that you like to talk a lot, and some people will love it. Some people will think it's too much that you want to spend all the time when you're not at work together, and other people will feel you are being a barrier to the other things that they like to do, such as hobbies or spending time with friends. To some people physical affection is a joy; to others it's an obligation. Consider not only what you're expecting but who you are expecting it from, and then ask yourself: *If these actions or qualities are not this person, do I still choose them?*

BUILDING BLOCK 4. COMMUNICATION

At some point in any relationship self-help book, the author will raise the key issue of communication. Our awareness of the significance of communication comes not only from lived experience but also from psychological science. People in a relationship with what they perceive as good communication report greater satisfaction with the relationship and a greater ability to resolve conflict.

You, like all of us, come to relationships with certain assumptions based on your life experiences. You and your partner or friend will have different perspectives, so a lack of communication can lead to greater conflict. How do you relate to conflict? How do you think about it? You may avoid conflict because you think avoidance keeps everyone peaceful and happy. You may create conflict and drama because you think that makes relationships exciting. You may enjoy engaging in conflict with the hopes that you if you both express everything, it will save the relationship.

Your style of dealing with conflict is important to consider. It is not just about the fact that you are communicating, but also about the manner in which you communicate. Does the other person feel interrogated or attacked? Can you create room for a mutual conversation, a dialogue in which both people feel heard? Here are some pointers for a positive communication dynamic in any relationship:

- Communicate regularly instead of waiting for a crisis or problem.
- Work on being both expressive and clear.
- Listen to understand the other person, not to defend your point.
- Ask clarifying questions when you're not sure.
- Don't yell, curse at, name-call, threaten, or seek to humiliate the other, or take up all of the conversation.
- Validate your partner's or friend's feelings and appreciate their willingness to share.
- Be honest in what you say, and don't strategically, intentionally leave out information that you know would have a bearing on the other person.
- Let love and respect guide your words, tone, and body language.

It's healing to be in relationship with people who desire to know you and want to work things out. You may have heard the term *fighting fair.* This means that when there is conflict, tension, or disagreement, you want to keep the issue as the focus of the problem instead of attacking the person. Try not to overgeneralize by saying "You always . . ." or "You never . . ." Unless it truly is a pattern that needs to be addressed, when we overgeneralize, it can cause the other person to feel that their efforts are not being acknowledged when there are times that they have made the positive choice. Share the specific issue, including how it made you feel and what, if anything, you would like to happen. Each of us is different and circumstances are different. Consider if you would like the person to give you space or if you would like to see them demonstrate effort in repairing the relationship. Would you like an apology? Would you like them to communicate back to you their understanding of why what they did was problematic or hurtful? Are you looking for a specific change in behavior, or do you want a certain behavior to stop? Would you like the two of you to attend counseling? Share what you would like. If you're not certain, you can be honest and say something along the lines of "Some people need space, and some people want you to fight for them or keep showing up." You can also be honest and say, "I don't know what will fix it, but I just know I'm not happy."

If you are the person who has hurt or offended your friend or partner, listen carefully to what they are sharing. Reflect on what was said, and then if you feel it sincerely, you may want to offer an apology without justifying or excusing your behavior. The best apology is a verbal acknowledgment of the harm that was done, followed by a change of behavior. If you have hurt someone, you don't get to create the timeline in which they must get over it. Healing ruptures can take time. Even if the person accepts your apology that same day, there may have been damage done to the trust and connection between you, which will need to be rebuilt.

BUILDING BLOCK 5.
GRACE AND FORGIVENESS

When you want to preserve the relationship, there will be times that you need to show grace and extend forgiveness. People are not perfect, and there will be times when someone will disappoint you. They will even disappoint themselves at times. Being gracious doesn't mean you to have to be silent or a doormat or a victim. You want to consider the overall relationship and the ways in which the other person demonstrates their care, love, and respect. Does the other person exhibit remorse or changes in behavior, or does everything continue as it was before?

Forgiveness doesn't mean that you forget. It also doesn't mean the actions were inconsequential. Forgiveness doesn't have to be instant. It is a process, one that can include a range of feelings from grief to anger to sadness. To forgive is to open yourself up to the choice to not allow the sting of the harm to dominate you or to keep you stuck. You may choose to free your heart from remaining in a state of active agitation. Know that forgiveness is not the same as reconciliation. Someone may forgive a relative or friend and still not spend the same amount of time with that person, especially if there is no evidence of transformation, meaning the harmful acts are likely to continue. In other instances, you may forgive a person who is authentically sorry, and the two of you may work together toward reconciliation.

Remember your aim in any conflict. If you want to address the issue but not dismantle the relationship or destroy the other person, you will choose your words and actions with that in mind. People remember what we said and how we made them feel even after much time has passed. Some conflicts can be resolved in one conversation, others may involve multiple conversations over time, and some can never be resolved completely, meaning one person will not get what they want and will need to make peace with this or decide that the relationship is too misaligned for it to continue. If there was or is love present, even in conflict you can choose to be gracious. To be gracious toward the other person *and* yourself is necessary so that you can be true to yourself and your values.

BUILDING BLOCK 6. FLEXIBILITY

You want to meet people where they are now, which means recognizing that they will change over time. People evolve over time: their interests change and they want new experiences. Flexibility is a gift you give to them and yourself. Growth and change are a part of life. People who are on healing journey may begin to speak up for themselves more, set different boundaries, and express new needs or desires. When you love someone, you support and encourage their transitions instead of blocking them. Appreciate who they are in the present, even if that is different from who they used to be. When positive changes happen to them, you want to be a supportive friend or partner.

At other times changes develop as a result of external challenges. A loved one may become overwhelmed, depressed, anxious, angry, or mournful as a result of a layoff, health issues, the death of a loved one, a big promotion, or a traumatic event. As a true friend, you want to show up for your friend or partner when they are not their usual funny, lighthearted, superstrong self. It is foundational for a healthy relationship that in your presence, people can become undone, honest, raw, human. Cultivate flexibility in your relationships so that you are the kind of person people can turn to for both celebrating their triumphs and grieving their disappointments.

BUILDING BLOCK 7. CO-CREATE JOY

Joyful moments keep fuel in the tank and water in the well of your relationship. Difficulties will crop up, and if you're already running on empty, it will be hard for one or both of you to feel there is something worth fighting for. Some people make the mistake of believing it is the other person's job to make them happy. You may have thought, *After I meet the one, when we start dating, after I fall in love, after we get married, after we have children,* then *this person will make me happy.* Joy is both an inside job for the individual and a collective job for the relationship. Do your part to bring joy to yourself, the other person, and the union. Put time and thought into creating joyful moments for you to do activities together that you enjoy.

A stand-up comedian once said there is a big difference between audience members who come ready to laugh and those who come with the mindset that you can't make them laugh. When you come out on the stage, one group is smiling, ready to enjoy themselves, and the other is smirking, daring you to entertain them. When your friend or partner comes into the room, do you greet them with a smile that says *I'm expecting to enjoy your company* or with a scowl that says *I'm already annoyed with you?* In psychology, we have a term called a *self-fulfilling prophecy.* Sometimes we create such a negative environment that the other person is responding to it. Be sure you are doing your part to co-create a joyful experience. A friend or partner should not carry the whole weight of bringing you happiness. Let it multiply. When you have joy in your heart and in your day and it comes in contact with their joy, the two of you can create a beautifully special connection.

Picture what it feels like when you see someone light up because they are happy to see you. When friends, siblings, or spouses are both joyful to see each other, the joy builds and grows. While you may not be joyful every day, especially when you are not having the best day, you can take intentional steps to bring joy to your relationship. Joy is not present only when life is perfect. In the African American tradition, we talk about joy anyhow, which means that even though I may be struggling in some areas, I can make a decision to hold on to my joy or to create some joy. The joy may not erase the despair, but it can coexist with the challenges. In other words, you may be grieving the loss of a parent and still enjoy that your partner is present with you as you both grieve. Even if money is tight, free time is limited, or dreams are deferred, I hope you can create some anyhow joy.

Joshua is in his late twenties and is realizing how much intellectual and emotional depth mean to him. He's been in a transition time of either transforming or letting go of his friendships. Previously, his friendship circle consisted of men who wanted to talk about nothing but sports or their sexual conquests. Joshua has been giving a lot of thought to the type of man he wants to be. He has been greatly influenced by an older mentor, who advised Joshua that the types of people he chooses to associate with can significantly shape his life. His mentor shared some bad decisions he made early in his life as a result of trying to impress the wrong people. Thinking about this, Joshua started to share more with his friends about his dreams, fears, hopes, and struggles. Some were unresponsive or even dismissive, but a few have gravitated toward more thoughtful conversations. Joshua is grateful for the brotherhood circle he is cultivating and feels that they are making each other better as they strive to better themselves.

ACTIVATION EXERCISE: Plan a joy-giving activity with a friend or partner. It doesn't have to be expensive. Invite your loved one to do something that could bring you both joy, preferably something that you don't already do all the time. If your usual evening is to watch television together, you could go for a walk instead or go to a coffee shop to talk. You could go to a concert or a painting class, or cook a meal together. Let the person know through your words, tone, and actions that you enjoy having them in your life.

AFFIRMATION: If it aligns with you, embrace yourself and affirm, "I am building healthy, loving connections in my life. My heart says yes."

5

KEYS TO A HEALTHY RELATIONSHIP

Richard and Camille are an African American couple in their seventies. When they first became a couple, Richard's mother didn't approve of his choice of a wife because Richard's family was middle class and Camille came from a poor family. Richard's friends thought Camille was too strong and independent thinking to be a good wife. Richard ignored all of them and followed his heart. He saw Camille's brilliance, beauty, and compassion and was confident that she was the person with whom he wanted to spend his life. His commitment didn't waver. Camille had not planned to share her life with someone who was religious, but when she spent time with Richard, she knew he was the person her heart wanted to journey with. Regardless of the differences in their expectations and despite the opposition of others, Richard and Camille have had to stretch and grow, but their hearts continue to sing a love song together after five decades.

While challenges in love may have drawn you to this book, *Matters of the Heart* is not just about addressing problems. It is also about building and protecting healthy relationships. To sustain a healthy relationship, you need to know both that such relationships exist and how you can go about recognizing the signs to look for and to develop. When you see these signs, they can serve as a green light to move forward. You are worthy of emotional and physical safety, which are key aspects of a healthy relationship.

A healthy relationship provides a good base, a foundation that enables you to grow and flourish. It's important for you think about the green lights or green flags in a relationship instead of considering only red flags or warning signs. When you look for nothing but red flags, you are perpetually trying to decide if you should leave. This may lead to your walking away quickly or prematurely. In any relationship, there will naturally be adjustments, and while you will see differences between the two of you, you also want to look for green lights, which create the capacity to address those differences and grow together.

I invite you to consider times in your life when you either had a healthy relationship or witnessed healthy—not perfect—relationships. You may have seen such relationships among family members or friends. It may have been when you were growing up, or perhaps you have had your own experiences in a healthy relationship. Even if you have not, you can learn a lot from considering the qualities of the relationships you have respected or admired. Consider the things you noticed or that stood out to you, the qualities in someone you encountered, dated, or were in a relationship with that made you feel like "this is a place where I can breathe, grow, and flourish."

I want to share some of the indicators of healthy relationships. These are based on the volumes of research on healthy relationships in the areas of psychology, marriage counseling, and family therapy, as well as intimacy and sexual pleasure.

CARING IS KEY

One of the green lights you want to think about is the heart of the person. Are they empathetic, compassionate, and caring, and are you empathetic, compassionate, and caring? When considering the health of a relationship, we need to think about more than how we feel about each other. Those feelings should then guide the ways in which we communicate and show up for each other, operating from a place of kindness and compassion. If the other person is uncaring toward you or you really don't care about them, the relationship is not going to be healthy.

In a healthy relationship, you care about each other's feelings, values, needs, and goals. You are able to grieve together and celebrate together. You are moved by the experiences of the other, and they are moved by your experiences. When you care about each other, you are observant and invested in learning about each other. You take the time and effort to learn what brings the other joy and a sense of being cared for and then engage in those actions routinely, not sporadically or inconsistently.

Kaito and Aya are a couple in their fifties. Aya was essentially raised by her mother, who actively loved and cared for her. While her father was physically present in the home, he was emotionally absent. She has always been attracted to men who were emotionally unavailable. The pattern of having to chase people and convince them that she was worthy of love was established early. In her early forties, after divorcing someone who was emotionally unavailable, she spent some time healing in therapy. She then met Kaito. She has been amazed at what it feels like to be cared for. Kaito pays attention to her words, facial expressions, and actions. He is attentive and affirming.

This relationship has been healing for Aya and has allowed her to soften and be more present with herself and with Kaito. The relationship has been healing for Kaito as well. He is divorced, too, and acknowledges that in his prior marriage he was selfish and stubborn. The combination of learning from what this prior behavior cost him and reflecting on the caring behaviors that his father, who is now deceased, demonstrated toward his mother has allowed him to show up as a loving partner. The two of them are healing and learning as they choose to be present and mindful to give each other compassion.

OPEN COMMUNICATION IS KEY

When you are in a relationship in which you can be your authentic self—in which you can express yourself, your feelings, and your thoughts—and the other person also feels safe and comfortable with you, this will foster a healthy relationship. Relationships with open communication allow you to grow together.

Open communication has a number of key components. It is proactive and not avoidant. When you and your partner have a concern, neither of you shuts down and becomes resentful of actions that your partner may not be aware of. It's better to share your thoughts, feelings, needs, and desires. When partners don't share, needs remain unfulfilled and resentment can grow. Communication should be based on love and respect, even when there is disagreement. Communication that is non-blaming, over-generalizing, or attacking is best for creating an environment where the other person feels comfortable sharing as well. Consider communication that is invitational instead of demands that may feel rooted in entitlement or hostility. Reflect on the ultimate goal of your sharing. If the aim is to build connection with the other person, then you will not use words, tones, or gestures that are humiliating or demeaning. An emotionally mature aspect of relational communication includes the ability to acknowledge wrongdoing and apologize with both words and a change of behavior.

Sometimes when I have given these tips to clients, people who have experienced harm in the past don't like the idea of needing to be kind. They associate kindness with weakness and abuse. Kindness is not the same as being silenced, and it is not the same as being a powerless victim. Kindness, respect, and love should be mutual; they become grounds for abuse only when you are with an abusive person. If you are in a relationship where you are mistreated whenever you are kind, this is not a healthy relationship. Someone who is caring will be responsive to your sharing your heart on a matter, even if they disagree. If you feel you have to become aggressive to be heard in your relationship, the relationship is not healthy. (If when you share an issue from your heart, it is ignored until you scream, curse, throw things, or hit someone, this is not a healthy relationship.) Cultivate relationships where you hear the heart of the other and where they hear you based in a mutual desire to understand and nourish each other. Consider if you are responding to your old script based on past relationships, or if in fact the new relationship is a repeat of old abusive dynamics.

SELF-AWARENESS IS KEY

Being self-reflective or self-aware is vital in creating and sustaining healthy relationships. When people do not know themselves, they can scarcely be aware of what they want in a relationship. They will also find it hard to take responsibility for their share of the issues or difficulties in the relationship. People who are not self-aware will often believe that they have always been perfect and that the person they are with now and others they have been in relationships with are the only ones at fault. When you are reflective, you're able to take note of ways you may have contributed to the problem and also things you can do that can create a healthier sense of connection. Ask yourself, what are your strengths in relationships, and what are the things that you need to work on? Do you consistently choose friends and dating partners who are unkind, uncaring, and neglectful? Do you find yourself drawn to people who demonstrate a fear of or disdain for commitment? Are you conflicted between what you say you want and how you act? Do you desire relationship and simultaneously engage in actions that are self-sabotaging or relationship sabotaging? Can you see yourself engaging in those actions as they are happening or before you do them, or can you not see what's going on until it is too late? What are your triggers? What bothers you the most in relationships and why? Have you communicated that to your partner? Are you able to recognize, own, and sort through your stuff instead of harming yourself and your partner with unhealthy habits? I invite you to see you, to sit with you, to be aware of yourself. This awareness will create a soft place for you to land and openness in your relationship.

Then consider the person you are getting to know or are in a relationship with. Are they exhibiting an awareness about themselves? Are they conscious of the truth about who they are and what their life experience has been? Do they have any awareness regarding ways in which their journey has shaped them and in which they may still need to heal and to grow? When you are in a relationship with someone who is self-aware and willing to reflect on themselves, there is an openness, ease, and breath to your time together instead of a sense of walking on eggshells.

GROWTH AND CHANGE ARE KEY

I'm sure you know that awareness without follow-through is insufficient. So reflect on what you have done to improve in areas where you seek to grow and transform. Be honest with yourself. Consider how motivated and sincere you are about the change process. In a healthy relationship, both people are maturing and enhancing their relationship. For a relationship that does not merely endure but soars, you want to be open, able to expand and grow. Have you seen growth in yourself and your partner in your communication style, in your emotional and physical intimacy, in your ability to resolve conflict, in your nourishment of yourself, and in your consideration of the other person? It will be challenging if one person is committed to staying in their current mindset and patterns and is not willing to grow and to change.

When you have people in a relationship who are not only self-aware but are investing time and energy into being their best selves, both for themselves and then also for the relationship, then you have a green light, an indication that this relationship has the possibility and the capacity to be sustainable. People don't have to be perfect to have a healthy relationship, but they need to demonstrate the ability to receive feedback, adjust, and grow. A new mindset or behavior will not always come easily, but change is possible when we are motivated to show up in healthier ways. With this in mind, try not to dismiss a change of behavior by saying, "Well, you're just doing that or saying that because I asked you to." Appreciate the effort people make in transforming as a result of your feedback or requests. For example, initially the person may not be used to checking in with anyone during the day. They may sincerely care about you but be used to not making contact when they're working. If you've asked for communication during the day and they now call or text to check on you, see this as a sign that they are willing to adjust to be attentive to your requests, needs, and desires. Growth and change can include stepping outside of your normal or natural patterns of behavior or speech to be responsive to the person you are with. Suppose you are an extrovert and your partner is socially anxious. Instead of planning to go out every weekend late into the night, the two of you may come to a compromise that honors both your enjoyment of socializing and their anxiety around socializing. This can take different forms, such as but not limited to (1) adjusting the number of outings, (2) adjusting the duration of the outings, or (3) attending some social events with a best friend to take the pressure off your socially anxious partner. Your partner might work on strategies like meditation to manage and decrease their anxiety or might attend more events than they would if they were single, but not stay until the end.

BOUNDARIES ARE KEY

You also want to think about the value of honoring boundaries and rules. What are the ways in which you respect each other and, as a result, honor each other's needs, requests, parameters, and limitations? If you say that you would really like to get some rest, is that need respected or honored? If you and your partner are arguing and your partner asks for a time-out or a pause to collect themselves, will you honor that? If you come home from a long day of work or some activity that is stressful to you and you indicate that you need some quiet time, is your partner willing and able to honor those requests? Whether emotional or physical, the expression of a boundary is a crucial communication, and honoring those expressions is a beautiful green light. Of course, the consideration needs to be mutual, especially when competing needs are being expressed. If your partner is home all day with the kids and really needs a break, you can't always say you had a stressful day at work and need alone time when you get home. In this situation, there will need to be a compromise to meet the needs of both partners—perhaps alternating days or times. A healthy relationship honors the needs of both people instead of one person's needs always being prioritized and the other's needs always being ignored.

Boundaries during conflict are also very important. I once had a client with a history of aggression in prior relationships. I recommended that in his new relationship he work on recognizing when his feelings were starting to build up in a way that felt out of control and then giving himself pause by going for a walk, meditating, journaling, or calling a friend. A few weeks later he found himself having a disagreement with his partner and felt his anger rising, so he said he needed to go for a drive and would return to finish the conversation. The partner experienced this as abandonment and blocked the door, refusing to let him leave. This was a tense moment. As long as someone is not engaging in persistent avoidance—an unwillingness to ever address issues—it is important to honor time and space for both people to have the emotional capacity to show up in a healthy way. Healthy boundaries and rules of engagement are established with respectful communication, ideally in moments when you are both calm and grounded. Some people like to process their thoughts by means of a conversation, and others prefer to reflect on their ideas and feelings before sharing. Be self-aware, communicate, and take into account the preferred communication style and emotional life of your partner, recognizing you may not have the same expectations, preferences, or experiences.

SHARED BELIEFS CAN BE KEY

For many people, another green light or positive sign is a partner who has a sense of spirituality, which may include the underlying belief that both the person and their partner are sacred and that the relationship itself is sacred. The specific form of spirituality may vary from couple to couple or even within the couple, but the spiritual aspect may include a sense of wonder and appreciation of a higher source, God, or life force that can provide wisdom and love. Both spiritual beliefs and practices can be nourishing. Spiritual practices can include meditating, praying, reading sacred texts, fasting, attending spiritual or religious services, or connecting to the sacred with the arts, nature, volunteerism, or advocacy. Sharing beliefs and practices can fortify you to show up for each other in meaningful ways, provide a common element of connection, and also provide relational guideposts to stay on a positive track or to get back on a positive track. Spirituality can be a bond that joins you, a source of accountability, and a set of shared values. It is valuable for both partners' spirituality to be cultivated and honored.

Joel and Michelle are a White couple in their thirties. They shared that they used to pray together and found it helpful, but given the demands of marriage, work, and parenthood, they found their joint prayers had become scarce. I asked how they would feel about starting each morning by waking up at the same time, saying a prayer, and reading an affirming scripture to set the tone for their day. They liked the idea and readily agreed on the time they would start the practice. At our next session I found out a large conflict had emerged from what was supposed to be their spiritual connection time. Joel believed that as the man he knew what the scriptures meant and that

Michelle should listen to his teaching. When she would offer her own interpretation, he took it as insulting, concluding that it meant she didn't trust or respect his role as the man of the house. We worked toward a healthy understanding that they could both contribute to the reflection time and expanded Joel's ideas of sacredness (by also addressing the underlying insecurity that made other ideas threatening).

VULNERABILITY IS KEY

It is also a healthy sign when people are able to have some level of vulnerability with each other. I hope you have an open, accepting, loving relationship within which you do not feel like you have to always perform or pretend. In a healthy relationship, your partner wants you to be honest. You can safely share your insecurities, doubts, fears, exhaustion, and uncertainties. You don't have to pretend that you're happy when you're not. You don't have to pretend that you're confident when you're not. You are worthy of a relationship where you don't have to pretend you have it all together when your world is falling apart. You can show your vulnerability, weaknesses, or limitations. In this healthy space, you can share your mistakes, failures, and disappointments. You don't have to engage in public relations or live on a stage. You can take off the mask and costume. You can have a sense of openness, feeling that truth-telling is welcomed and appreciated. Likewise, your partner doesn't have to promote the image of themselves as invincible or always happy.

Valerie and Ayo have been dating for two years. Valerie was born in and grew up in the United States. Ayo was born in West Africa and immigrated as an adult. While Ayo makes a solid middle-income salary, owns a home, and gives Valerie thoughtful gifts, she notices his stress around money. They have been dating for over a year before Ayo shares his financial obligations for his extended family back home. He notes that other American women he has dated were not understanding of his responsibility to help his relatives who have not had the opportunities that he has. He took the risk of sharing, and Valerie is supportive and becomes a safe place for him to discuss his decision-making, guilt, and limit-setting, as the requests are sometimes massive and beyond his capacity. The open sharing and vulnerability create a greater understanding between them.

OUTSIDE HEALTHY CONNECTIONS

Another possible good sign in your relationship is when both of you have had healthy friendships and some healthy family connections. Some of the same qualities that allow you to sustain friendships or family connections over the years can be of service to you in a romantic relationship. There are some people in your life who have stood the test of time. There are skills required to sustain friendships or family relationships—communication, conflict resolution, and grace extended for our imperfections as human beings. Reflect for yourself and to observe with your partner both of your abilities and challenges with friendship and family. Take notice of what the presence or absence of these relationships may indicate. Consider what you have actively said or done to nourish those relationships. Consider if there are lessons to be learned from the friendships or family relationships that you did not maintain. Of course, some unhealthy relationships may have needed to end, but if you have not been able to maintain *any* connections, consider what mindsets and skills you or your partner may need to develop for this relationship to work.

I encourage you to think about not only the existence of these relationships but the healthiness of these connections. Are your closest friends and relatives people who encourage your growth and healthy decision-making, or have you grown in spite of their negative influence? If you have a circle of close friends who all treat their partners badly and encourage you to do the same, this is not a healthy launching pad for your relational life. Likewise, if you're close to your family but they always make you feel as though you have to choose them over your dating partner, this will also create difficulty. True friends and relatives will encourage you to be your best self, including in your relationships. They won't always take your side, especially when you are wrong. Good friends and family can help you see yourself, show up better in your relationships, and grow in healthy ways.

APPRECIATION IS KEY

Another quality to look for is appreciation. In a healthy relationship, you don't take each other for granted. When you both verbally express appreciation and demonstrate appreciation in your actions, you will feel more connected. When you sense that in this person's presence, you feel emotionally secure, you will be at ease to soften toward them and show up fully. You feel that this person has made you a priority, enjoys the real you, and isn't seeking to harm you but to nourish you. When you are in the presence of someone who appreciates you, you don't feel confused, disrespected, or dismissed. Your relationship is nourishing, validating, accepting, and loving. An appreciative partner is not warm one day and cold the next. An appreciative partner expresses their appreciation in your love language, and you do the same. Whether your special love language is time, verbal affirmation, tasks, gifts, or physical affection, you feel loved by them and they feel loved by you. When you appreciate each other, you have clarity and ease in the relationship instead of stress and insecurity. (As a reminder, if those feelings of insecurity aren't derived from the current relationship but are rooted in events of the past, you must work through those issues so they do not sabotage the relationship.)

SAFETY IS KEY

When was the last time you felt safe in someone's presence? Do you feel you can trust your partner's words, actions, and intentions? In a healthy relationship, you do not have to brace yourself emotionally or physically for your partner's harmful actions. They take your safety and well-being into consideration and do not act maliciously or carelessly toward you. Your partner is thoughtful about the impact of their actions on you, and you in turn are thoughtful and considerate of them. The basis of the relationship is love, not fear. You are not perpetually afraid that they will hurt, leave, or reject you. You do not have to make excuses or second-guess your relationship. Whether they are with you or elsewhere, you feel your heart is safe with them. Whether you are alone or in a crowded room, you feel your heart is well cared for. Whether you are having the best moment of your life or facing the worst devastation of your life, you feel you are safe to share your truth with them. Emotional and physical safety are necessary for a sustainable, healthy relationship.

INVESTMENT IS KEY

Neglect can kill a relationship. In a healthy relationship, you and your partner are equally invested. When there is difficulty, you both try to work things out, whether that is putting time in for communication, for working through conflict, or just for enjoying each other's company. Time, energy, and effort give people a sense of security. It's clear that you both have a vested interest in seeing the relationship blossom and grow.

We need emotional investment, especially now. People are under a lot of pressure and are increasingly overwhelmed by the demands of work and life, and mental health resources are stretched thin. In this context, it can be even easier to grow apart when a relationship is not nourished. In a healthy relationship, even when time is limited, you feel that the person is still invested in you, and you likewise are still invested in them. When time and energy are limited, simply be thoughtful. Consider some ways your partner has expressed a need or desire that you could support in this season.

BALANCE: INDEPENDENCE AND CONNECTION ARE KEY

In a healthy relationship, both people nourish themselves. When you enter a relationship, this doesn't mean you can now leave it to the other person to take care of all of your needs and wants. The things you used to do for your self-care should continue. To sustain a healthy relationship, you need to be healthy and whole yourself. Do not lose yourself in a relationship. Your identity is the foundation of who you are and is the basis of any relationship you form with anyone else. Remember your hobbies, interests, dreams, work goals, health plan, family, and friends. Some studies have found that in relationships men feel happier and more cared for, while women feel more stressed and neglected. Both partners should engage in self-care and care for the other.

Having a full, balanced life is important for both of you. When you do not abandon yourself, you will not feel resentful or envious when your partner practices self-care. In a healthy relationship, especially in a situation including children, you will need to be intentional about sacrifice and the sharing of responsibilities so both partners can have their needs met. What were the things that used to make you come alive? What brings you joy? When you make your partner the sole source of your joy, that is a heavy weight, which is not fair to either of you. In a healthy relationship, you spend time connecting with each other, but you also reclaim yourself and your interests. You may be in a book club and your partner may have a hiking group. You may have a monthly meal with friends and your partner may do the same. You may go on an annual women's retreat and your partner may go to a tennis tournament. One of you may decide to go back to school and the other may enjoy volunteering at a shelter. You don't have to do every activity together. Each relationship is unique, *and* it is healthy for both people to be whole people. These practices allow you to show up for each other fulfilled, joyful, inspired, and balanced. With this in mind, instead of seeing self-care activities or interests as burdensome or threatening, you encourage each other and celebrate each other for being your full selves.

AFFECTION IS KEY

Another green light or positive sign is affection. I've mentioned appreciation, but affection is also important. Someone may appreciate who you are and what you do but still show little affection. For a relationship to feel nourishing, it should involve some form of affection. In a healthy relationship, you and your partner express your care for each other. Affection and intimacy are central aspects of connection. You can show affection with touch, and the touch doesn't have to be sexualized. A kiss, a hug, cuddling, holding hands, a massage, and even a loving caress when you are walking past can be beautiful signs of affection.

In a romantic relationship, both people need to feel that they are seen, attractive, and desired. The way you express that may vary based on your personality, comfort, history, and body image. If it feels tough for you, now is the time to develop a language for affection and intimacy. We will discuss this in greater detail in a later chapter. For now, think about the ways you show affection, as well as emotional and physical intimacy. If you operate more like roommates than partners, it is likely that one or both of you are not having their relationship needs met. When you have an affectionate partner and you are affectionate as well, the relationship can feel well watered and sustained. Simple acts can revive passion and connection. Consider the level of affection in your current relationship, or if you are single, consider the level of affection you would desire in a relationship. It is important to know this about yourself and to communicate it, while also hearing the heart of your partner. Affection is a dance that changes over time but keeps you in flow with your partner.

FUN IS KEY

While you probably have heard that relationships are work, and they are, remember that healthy relationships can also be a source of fun. Some people mistakenly associate a spouse or committed partner with obligation, duty, and work, while associating secretive affairs involving no commitments with fun. When you're in a long-term relationship, you sometimes get so focused on the obligations, duties, and bills that you can lose sight of the basics. Aim to enjoy each other's company and maintain your friendship, reclaim your friendship, or develop a friendship within the relationship. In a healthy relationship, you don't avoid hard topics, but you also ensure that every conversation isn't an argument or full of conflict and tension. Having fun together doesn't require a grand occasion with a large budget. It can be as simple as talking and laughing as you take a walk, watch a show, play a game, clean up together after dinner, or go to a concert. Fun is not just about what you are doing but about who you are doing it with. If you have now or have ever had a best friend, think about what you did together that was fun. It may have been running errands or talking on the phone or meeting after work. In a healthy relationship, your partner is your friend and you enjoy spending time with them. It is healthy and nourishing for you to be playful together. Laughing and joking puts fuel in the tank. It allows you to keep going and gives you energy and the necessary motivation to continue to invest in the relationship. Every moment won't be lighthearted, of course, but try to be intentional about bringing some lightness to each other's lives. This can mean sending a funny or flirty text in the middle of the day or taking time to reflect together on fun moments in the past. Joy is a part of healthy relationships.

SUPPORT IS KEY

In a healthy relationship, you respect and support your partner and their dreams. When I care about you and your dreams, I am a supporter, an advocate, and a cheerleader, and I take actions in service of those dreams. This can take many forms, depending on the dreams and the individuals. Support may involve listening, sharing feedback when requested, making a sacrifice to support the dream, and looking for ways to help make the dream come true. In a healthy relationship, you are both supportive. You are the wind beneath each other's wings. Sometimes time and finances are challenging, but ultimately you both want each other to win. For example, it may not work for you both to leave your jobs and go to school at the same time, but you are thoughtful about when, not if, the person who waits will have their dream supported in turn.

A healthy relationship is not a competition. You both sincerely and authentically want the other person to have a fulfilling life. You are mutually of service to each other. You each see the other's dreams and abilities not as a threat to the relationship but as a vital part of the person, worthy of nourishing.

> *Alicia and José are a Latino couple in their twenties. She teaches dance at a middle school and wants to open a dance studio in the community she grew up in. He wants to work his way up to manager at the store where he is employed. They stay up at night discussing these dreams: the business plan for the studio and the strategy to become manager. Their enthusiasm for each other's dreams is evident and consistent. You can see the pride and admiration they have for each other and about what they will do. José works some extra shifts so they can save up for the studio, and Alicia encourages José to advocate for himself at work when new opportunities open up. They have their own dreams while their hearts are singing together.*

I invite you to consider all of these factors as you seek to build and cultivate a healthy relationship. In the following chapters, I will unpack some of these themes further and will introduce some new concepts as well. I'm excited about your healed and growing heart, as well as the connections you will nourish.

ACTIVATION EXERCISE: Sometimes when you think about relationships as something to build or fix, you can forget to enjoy the person you're connected to. This week, plan a fun activity together. Try to pick something that both of you will enjoy. This can help you both remember why the connection is worth nourishing and prioritizing. Shared laughter strengthens your bond. Enjoy each other.

AFFIRMATION: If it aligns with you, place one or both hands on your heart and declare, "I am worthy of giving and receiving love."

6

BEING MORE
EMOTIONALLY AVAILABLE

———————————

For any relationship to thrive, you and your family member, friend, or partner must be emotionally available. The qualities you want to strengthen include being emotionally present, emotionally stable, able to communicate effectively, able to understand the other's feelings and perspective even if you don't agree, good at listening, and capable of conveying a sense of security, consistency, and reliability.

Are you emotionally available? In other words, are you able to build and maintain a healthy emotional connection? Can you express your emotions accurately and be responsive to your partner's emotions? On the other hand, does your fear of intimacy or commitment make it difficult for you to connect, which results in your pulling away? I want to note that if any of these signs are a result of your neurodiversity, I don't mean to shame or blame you. I encourage you to set goals that are in alignment with your knowledge of yourself.

If you have difficulty building or maintaining connections over time, consider what makes you block deeper connection. You may find something about being open and known frightening.

Perhaps earlier experiences or messages taught you to keep people out, and as a result, your connections tend to be superficial. You may know a lot of people but reveal very little about yourself to them. People may feel they have access to only a controlled part of you, while the core of you is contained, censored, and not free. Consider in this moment if there are parts of you that you hold back for fear of rejection or judgment. Are you hiding your faith, childhood wounds, financial situation, health condition, sexuality, or relationship status (pretending to be single, etc.)? Do you hide your emotions when you're sad, angry, embarrassed, confused, excited, or proud of yourself?

Authentic connections are those that don't require performance or public relations. You can show up as your true self and receive the truth of another. Be mindful of how often you feel you are showing only a fraction of yourself. Consider the thoughts, feelings, or experiences that taught you to keep your walls up. You may feel emotionally safer when people find it hard to read you, understand you, or connect with you. To tend to your heart includes changing the behaviors that make it hard for you to connect with others—actions that render you reserved, distant, and disconnected. But healing is possible; there is hope for you to have deeper connection and intimacy.

William is a bisexual married man in his forties with three children. While William was growing up, his father was emotionally distant and his mother sexually objectified him. When he got to college, he was mentored by young men who showed and told him that the measure of his manhood was in the number of people he could seduce. He learned to be charismatic and manipulative, becoming a different person for each woman. With his male friends, the exchanges were all based on drinking, watching sports, and sharing stories about sexual con-

quests. He never explored or discovered himself. Now at this point in his journey, with a successful business and an empty marriage, he is trying to figure out how to show up for himself and his wife.

I invite you to consider when and why you began checking out emotionally. As was true with William, did your parents or caretakers model emotional distance and disconnection? You might have perceived their coldness as strength. Perhaps they always put on a brave face as a way of not being present or of protecting themselves from perceived or actual vulnerability. You may also have experienced friendships, family relationships, or romantic relationships in which it was not safe for you to feel or express your emotions. You may have had partners who belittled you, ridiculed you, and insulted you in your presence or behind your back, when you were alone with them or even in the presence of others. You may have learned that the only way to survive the psychological assaults was to check out, disconnect, grow numb, dissociate, and convince them and yourself that none of it mattered. I am here, precious soul, to tell your heart does matter—your life integrity matters. When childhood or adulthood experiences taught you that you can never rely on anyone, I am here to say that cultivating healthy relationships means risking laying down your armor and deciding you no longer want to be a one-person army—one soldier against the world.

This would be a good moment to take a breath. You don't want to or have to go through life defending yourself against everyone all the time, hiding from everyone all the time. You may have grown up feeling you had the weight of the world on your shoulders, whether from having a parent with untreated mental illness, living in an unsafe home or neighborhood, or consistently receiving the message that perfection was required. These types of pressure keep you rigid and always observing yourself from the outside and prioritizing what others think of you over what you know of yourself. For a healthy connection, you will need to open the parts of you that you were taught, directly or indirectly, to keep closed.

Here are some signs that you may be emotionally unavailable:

- You haven't had a close friend or a long-term committed relationship.
- You feel uncomfortable sharing your feelings or experiences.
- You find verbal or physical affection uncomfortable or awkward.
- You never make time for people. You have organized your life in such a way that there is no space for connection.
- You don't share with others information about your life, friends, work, hobbies, etc.
- You think emotions are a sign of weakness.
- You have a pattern of being attracted to people who are unavailable (married, long-distance, or emotionally distant) because it protects you from having to be known, available, and seen.
- People get upset with you for sending mixed signals. Your words and actions don't align.
- You require perfection from people, and thus are quick to pull away and end connections.
- You are defensive and combative or shut down when others share their feelings.
- You don't put in the same amount of effort that others do in friendships or romantic relationships.

- You refuse to be "pressed," considering it a badge of honor not to be invested in or care about the outcome of your relationships.

In marriage or in romantic relationships involving cohabitation, emotional unavailability can also show up as taking your partner for granted, treating your partner more like a roommate or sibling, or treating them as an obligation, duty, or responsibility without care or (com)passion. This emotional unavailability can also lead to your keeping secrets, not spending time with them, or being physically present but emotionally absent.

I want to name that you may have chosen emotionally unavailability as a result of observing or being taught the dangers of emotional flooding. If you have seen a parent or loved one often become emotionally overwhelmed, you may have concluded, consciously or not, that it is safer not to have feelings. You may have falsely concluded that being logical, with no awareness of your emotions, was the best way to proceed. You may be puzzled when people complain that you are heartless, categorizing this as if it is a problem when you thought it was the solution. You may likewise associate feelings with weakness or the sense of being out of control and thus hold yourself tightly, emotionally and physically. This holding back shows up not just in your professional life but also your personal life. It is a barrier between you and those you love.

I also invite you to consider if you were taught that certain feelings were unacceptable or that no one cared what you feel. Let me acknowledge the truth of your experience. You may have been raised by people or gone to school with people or even dated or married people who think your heart doesn't matter. They are incorrect. Your feelings are important.

Additionally, you may be someone who was not always emotionally unavailable. Perhaps you used to feel things deeply. You were even called sensitive. You felt you were drowning in your emotions and it cost you. You were hurt, anxious, panicked, or stuck, and you don't want to go back there. You can feel your feelings without always drowning in them.

You may also have a fear of rejection that leads you to reject people first, dilute your emotions for fear of being too much, or pretend you have it all together. May you find places where your heart is safe to be expressive and expansive. You are not too much, and those who are for you find it an honor to show up with you in honest, authentic spaces.

Finally, I want to acknowledge that some of your emotional unavailability may have developed after you opened up to someone who subsequently left, abandoned, or cheated on you. All of this was painful and has taken time to heal. The conclusion of your healing journey is not about self-isolation and hyperindependence. An aspect of your healing will be softening your heart and reopening it after your season of being walled off for your own protection and preservation. I am happy to offer some pointers about becoming more emotional available.

GROWTH POINT— CONSIDER ALTERNATE ENDINGS

You may close yourself off because you see it as the only possibility that makes sense, given your past hurts. You may be engaging in what psychologists refer to as overgeneralization. When bad things have happened in your relationships in the past, you shut down to protect yourself from it happening again. As a child you may remember reading the books that allowed you to pick your own ending. At various choice points, you could decide for the character, and based on your decisions, the book ends a different way. Rejection, abandonment, and hurt are not the only endings if you choose to open up. You could be understood, appreciated, accepted, loved, chosen, affirmed, and desired as a result. Opening up can be the pathway to a deeper love instead of resulting in harm or ending a relationship. Instead of focusing so much on what openness and honesty can cost you, consider what you might gain.

Additionally, emotional availability is also about showing up for another person. If when someone cries or shows vulnerability, you get mad or distant, you have written a script about what their sharing their pain means about you. What if you did not take their sharing as an insult, an offense, or an attack? What else might it mean that someone is being vulnerable with you? You can create an alternate ending by showing up for them differently. Your attentive listening, lack of defensiveness, curiosity about their perspective, and concern for their heart as well as your own could lead you both to a deeper, more fulfilling place of intimacy.

GROWTH POINT—MEMORY LANE

Try to recall times that you were emotionally present for yourself and for others. Often you remember only the wall, the disconnection, and this can lead you to falsely conclude you're not capable of being present in a relationship or friendship. The truth is, no matter how long ago it happened or how rare it was, there have been times that your heart was open and that you even expressed it. There were times that you tuned in to the heart of another person and responded with care and compassion. Perhaps it was a childhood friend, a cousin, a favorite teacher, a first crush, a work best friend, or someone you saw struggling and offered encouragement to. It helps to know that you are not starting from scratch or ground zero. There may even be examples from your current relationship. Perhaps when you were first getting to know each other or before some painful event occurred, you were more present. If you have decided to work to repair and restore the connection, try remembering what it was like when you were more open to each other. Instead of solely thinking of the negative outcomes, recall the times when the dynamic or exchange was improved because of the condition of your heart and spirit. As you reflect on the past and begin to recover some of that capacity, be patient with yourself. You may find yourself triggered and self-doubting when you imagine the worst outcomes. You may even feel that you are incapable and unworthy of good love. The truth is that love is not just for the perfect. Love is not just for those who find it easy to open up. Love is for you, too. Give yourself permission to reclaim your prior wisdom and build new skills.

GROWTH POINT—
CONSIDER MODERATIONS

You may think in extremes about matters of the heart. You may think of people who are emotionally available as being open books or blabbermouths, having no boundaries, or sharing too much too soon and with too many people. You may think of people who are volatile or highly sensitive. In your desire to not be them, you may have chosen the other extreme. I invite you to reflect on a range of emotional experiences and expressions instead of adopting a false dichotomy between being "a mess" and being a wall. You can think about what it would look like for you to be more open to the feelings of your family members, friends, or partner, and to your own emotions. Perhaps instead of cutting off difficult conversations, you can ask more questions, share what you are feeling, write them a letter, or ask if you can continue the conversation after you have had time to think about it. It may help you to think about someone you admire who feels present overall, especially when you are sharing matters of your heart.

> *Michelle is a married woman who grew up in a household with domestic violence. Her father emotionally and physically abused her mother. Michelle identified her father as the one with power and control and modeled her relationships after him. Throughout her late teens and twenties, she manipulated men and was insincere and verbally abusive toward her partners. She would tell them that they were physically or financially inadequate. At the same time, they felt a sense of accomplishment for gaining access to her. Michelle associates emotions with victimhood, and she is determined not to be a victim. Her mother did not have the ability or safety to show up for herself or Michelle. Her father perpetually put her mother down and brought many women around Michelle—women he cheated with and was also abusive toward. Michelle recently married a wealthy, controlling man who is similar to her father. She is having trouble showing up for herself and her relationship. As hard as she fought not to be her mother, she feels powerless in the marriage and copes with the confusion with substance abuse, which of course creates more confusion.*

To have healthier emotional expression, you will need to develop your capacity to tell yourself the truth, to heal your past wounds, and to distinguish the past from the present so you don't end up participating in cycles you were trying to avoid.

GROWTH POINT—TAKE INITIATIVE

A part of emotional availability is being responsive, but it also entails taking the initiative to create opportunities for deeper connection. Instead of just waiting for people to ask the right question and then trying to share more authentically, consider bringing up a topic that is important to you. Instead of waiting for someone to ask you how you feel about them, have the courage and compassion to share what that person's friendship means to you. Instead of waiting for someone to share how you hurt their feelings, if you are already aware of what you have done, proactively engage with that person about the hurtful comment or action. Whether cultivating romance or repairing ruptures, you can take the lead instead of always running, shutting down, or using humor as a defense strategy. When you're not sure of what to say or you feel uncertain about the situation, you can even share that. Imagine shifting so that your friend or partner does not always have to be the person who pursues you, while you distance yourself hoping to be chased. Choose presence over performance and openness over closedness. Initiating dialogue, affection, and quality time are ways you can demonstrate your investment and availability.

GROWTH POINT—
NOTICE YOUR PATTERNS

When people get close to you, how do you usually sabotage it? To grow more emotionally available, you want to notice your patterns of distancing and interrupt them. You may notice that when your feelings are hurt or when you feel anxious about the possibility of being abandoned or rejected, you start to engage in destructive behaviors. You are hoping to cut the person off before they leave you. You may quickly resort to insults, threats to leave, silence, behavior that makes them jealous, or hostility. Notice your pattern. Are you punishing this person for something a previous person did? Does your reaction signal a deeper fear? Notice yourself closing off and resist that tendency. Choose to show up differently. It will feel uncomfortable, but that is the feeling of growing pains. You can grow into new choices and see the benefits of emotional presence instead of emotion retreat. I understand that your life experiences have led you to always brace yourself for bad outcomes. You may have developed a style of trying to hurt people before they hurt you. In this season, reclaim your courage and voice, as you will need both to engage. It doesn't mean every relationship or friendship is for you, but you want to participate fully so you can find out. Instead of threatening to leave at the first sign of a difference of opinion, take a breath and lean in for a deeper conversation. If departing is easy for you, emotionally or physically, your growth point may be learning how to stay present even when you're uncertain of the outcome. Some ruptures can heal. Even if in the long run, this friendship or relationship ends, you will have stayed long enough to learn more about yourself and your capacity to be present with another.

If you want intimacy, connection, and the sweetness of love, sometimes that requires pushing past your own programming, style, and patterns. The way you have protected yourself for years because of your wounds requires choosing yourself and choosing people with whom you can lay down your armor. Outlast the awkwardness instead of resorting to old patterns.

Ebony and Vivian are in a loving same-gender relationship. Ebony has never had a partner whom she felt genuinely cared for her. She was always uncertain of her prior partner's love and as a result perpetually overextended herself with hopes that the person would stay. When it came to intimacy, she would either emotionally check out due to her anxiety or resort to drinking to present herself as engaged and expressive. The couple worked in counseling for Ebony to know that in this relationship it was safe for her to show up fully, without being under the influence of substances. She has been pleasantly surprised by Vivian's care and her own ability to be present for a love that in the past would have felt too good to be true.

ACTIVATION EXERCISE: Set an intention to show up more emotionally open. If your guiding mantra is "I don't want to be hurt," all your actions are focused on not being known. In this moment, decide what you want your leading intention to be. It may be "I want to have spaces where I am open," "I want to be known and know another," or "I want authentic love." Your intention or mantra can then direct your actions toward greater emotional availability, presence, and genuine connection.

AFFIRMATION: If it aligns with you, place both palms face up on your lap as you declare aloud, "I choose to show up for myself and those I love with an open heart. I'm present."

7

MOVING FROM PASSIVE TO ASSERTIVE

Mai is in her thirties. She is in a new relationship and is both excited and anxious about it. Her prior relationship was emotionally and sexually abusive. She also grew up with a narcissistic mother who was physically, verbally, and emotionally abusive. There are questions she avoids asking and opinions she avoids disclosing to her new partner because she is afraid of being "too much." While it has been healing for her to express herself in therapy and discover that I will not abandon her, it has been especially liberating and healing for her to begin to express herself more openly with her partner and experience his understanding and acceptance when she expected abandonment and hostility.

Beloved, it's time to reclaim your relationships, which means you also need to reclaim your voice. This chapter is meant to enable you to move from passive to assertive, from silenced to empowered to use your voice. When stress and trauma disconnect you from yourself, you often lose your voice. In your love life, friendships, and family relations, consider the times you have abandoned yourself by not speaking the truth about your needs and wants. Your fear of being rejected or judged may have caused you to erase yourself. I'm so happy for you because now that you have begun this journey of attending to your heart, being silenced in relationships is no longer acceptable or tolerable. You want to invest only in healthy relationships in which you are free to be yourself. Moving from passive to assertive in relational communications is liberating, and you are worthy of a liberated love life.

You need to recognize the internal and external barriers you have faced that have hindered you from living in truth. Stress, trauma, and oppression may have taught you to censor, filter, and dilute yourself. You have shown up as a watered-down version of yourself because you thought this is what love looks like. It's time for you to awaken your voice and show up as yourself. If you are not truly present, you don't have authentic relationships. In this season, you do not want just the appearance of love. You want the real thing, which means you have to be real—a person with a voice.

In real love, you can show up in the fullness of who you are instead of being silenced and censored by the fear of disapproval. It's time for you to recognize the sound of your own voice. You are not just an echo of your partner, friend, or family member. You have your own voice. Sometimes you have just lost connection with yourself, but you can reclaim yourself, including your voice. Begin to consider what the true sound of your own sorrows, joys, fears, hopes, and thoughts is. What is the sound that reflects your true state of being?

In dysfunctional relationships, your voice didn't matter. For healthy love, you need to make room for truth to come out of your mouth. Authentic love requires an authentic voice. I invite you to get still enough, self-aware enough to recognize the voice within, and then share that voice with those you love.

Notice our aim is shifting from passive to assertive, not aggressive. When people are aggressive, they dominate and monopolize the space. They are prone to harassing others, bullying, and exhibiting other controlling behaviors. When you are assertive, you are comfortable speaking, but you also want to hear from others, even when their perspective is different from yours.

Whenever you think about shifting or changing, start by assessing where you are now and how you landed there. Think about what led you to be silent in relationships. Recognizing your earlier points in the journey can empower you to navigate your next steps.

You may be silent in relationships because of a lack of confidence. Reflect on what took your confidence. Do you not have a lot of prior relationship experience, so you assume your older or more experienced partner must know best? Maybe you were discouraged from speaking or ridiculed for your ideas in childhood or in prior friendships and relationships. When did you lose your fire, your freedom? To help you remember, think back to when you were more of a free spirit. Was there one event or many that led you to shut down? As you recall that time, you may become aware of some negative thoughts that developed about yourself or about relationships. You want to nourish the hurt heart that you carry while also giving yourself permission to build confidence in your voice, ideas, and feelings.

You may also have had the experience of being silenced at such an early age that you don't recall a time when you were free to express yourself. In your earliest memories, you may have already been silenced in your home, at school, or in your community.

Marlo is an Afro-Latino in his late twenties. He is smart, warm, gifted, and observant. He always did well in school, posting the highest marks in his grade. He noticed in high school that his excellence made some people envious and hostile, resulting in their rejecting him. He began holding back. He wouldn't raise his hand even though he knew the answer. He wouldn't put all of the answers he knew on tests, so other people had the opportunity to be the top. His strategy worked. More people began to approach him, engage with him, and like him. Now that he is in the professional world, he downplays his abilities with work and nonwork friends, just to make others comfortable. In dating, he doesn't like to share what he does or even ideas he has for fear of being off-putting or unapproachable. Marlo has lost his voice and doesn't have any relationships that are really built on truth.

Whether this is a new experience or one you have had to contend with your entire life, this is your reclamation season—the season you either reclaim the voice and free spirit you used to have or claim your voice for the first time. You don't need to spend the rest of your years silenced in your relationships.

You don't have to keep being disappointed and having partners or friends who are frustrated because you expect them to guess what you want or need. You no longer have to engage with people with the assumption that their needs or wants are the only thing that matter. You no longer have to use silence, games, manipulation, or emotional outbursts in place of expressing yourself sooner and more clearly. Voicing your needs and expressing your feelings does not have to be a last resort but instead can be a routine part of your loving relationships.

In addition to traumatic early events, two fears may have resulted in your being passive in your relationships.

FEAR OF DISAGREEMENT

Gerald is a married African American man in his forties. He realizes that a large part of what has shaped his interactions with his wife is that his mother made more money than his fa-

ther, and whenever his mother voiced a difference of opinion, his father perceived it as disrespect and an attack on his manhood. Gerald and his mom used to be puzzled by this response, and a large part of his childhood was spent anxiously anticipating the next time his father would blow up. Over time, his mother got quieter and more withdrawn. Gerald is intentional about always wanting to hear his wife's perspective and tries to create a dynamic in their marriage where her voice is as welcome as his own.

You may have had abusive relationships or grown up seeing partner abuse. From that exposure, you have concluded that disagreement always end in trauma, drama, and even violence. You may have experienced or witnessed people being punished for speaking up. As a result, you may approach all your interactions with the aim of people-pleasing. Your fear of disagreement and conflict drives your need to have everyone like, validate, and approve of you. Or quite simply, you might just like to keep the peace. You want everyone to be happy. I invite you to consider if your happiness and peace are important, too. I used to stay silent in relationships because I thought I was keeping the peace, but I finally had to ask myself whose peace I was keeping. The other person was at peace, but I was experiencing a suppressed war. Peace at the cost of your voice and feelings is not authentic peace; it's just silence. A liberated love is not rooted in fear or silence, but in the freedom for everyone to be the truest version of themselves.

FEAR OF ABANDONMENT

Childhood experiences or early relationship experiences may have driven you to the belief that if you are agreeable enough, silent enough, people won't leave you. You are silenced because of a fear of abandonment. But if you have to leave yourself, abandon yourself, for them to stay, the relationship has already cost you too much.

Genuine love is available, and to get to it, you have to let false love go. Anyone who doesn't want to be with the truth of you is not intended to be in your life. If they chose you based on a lie, they haven't chosen you. The truth is, you have opinions, fears, needs, wants, dreams, hopes, and some baggage. That is the truth of our humanity. Real connection requires that you are allowed to show up as your real self. If people leave because of something you share about yourself, they were not meant to be with you. You are worthy of a love that chooses you—the real you.

You may have also been silenced due to oppression. You may have received direct or indirect messages that you should be silent because of cultural scripts, gender scripts, and religious scripts. You may have been made to feel that your lack of education or your low income means that you should just be glad you were chosen and keep your mouth shut. You may also have been told that because of your youth, you haven't got anything worthwhile to say, or because you are older, you should be grateful that anyone wants to spend time with you. Whatever the conditioning that taught you that your voice is not valued, I invite you to consider the quality of any relationship based on forced silence. Any authentic love relationship, romantic or platonic, should be based on truth, regardless of your identity or demographics. People who care about you will want to know what you think and feel. Build those relationships. You're worthy.

Finally, some of you may have become silenced because you're trying so hard not to be what you witnessed growing up. You may have had controlling, abusive people in your family or community. In your desire not to emulate them, perhaps you have gone to the other extreme: silence and people-pleasing. In trying not to abuse others, you end up abandoning and harming yourself. You agree to things you don't want to do. You go along with dishonorable circumstances. You pretend not to care about things that break your heart. To nourish your heart and build healthier relationships, you need to discover that there is a world of options between being abusive and erasing yourself. It's time to explore the range of ways that allow you to be present with others without being harmful to them or yourself.

So the question before you now is how to be more assertive.

The first is to begin to pay attention to yourself. Self-awareness is key because you cannot express yourself if you don't know yourself. Explore your voice instead of always saying

I don't know.

I don't care.

It doesn't matter to me.

Whatever you want.

There are some things you do know, care about, and want. You may think silencing yourself is being kind, but you are robbing your friend or partner from getting to know you, and you are robbing yourself of the opportunity to be known. Kindness should not be a cover for self-erasure. You can experiment with giving your family, friends, and partner more truthful, revealing information instead of suppressing your thoughts or making people labor to find out what you think or want. You can make a goal of trying to more assertive, vocal, honest, and open in your communication.

The second strategy that can be helpful is to observe role models. Pay attention to how you see other people showing up and speaking up in their relationships. How do your partner, friends, and family members express themselves? Notice people who seem to have a healthy relationship—whether romantic, friendship, or family. Be mindful of the information they share with each other, the way they speak to each other, and the frequency of their sharing. There are different styles and personalities, but people in healthy relationships are enjoying direct communication.

You may notice that some people seem to be naturals at communicating, while others may confide in you or reveal to you that they have had to work at it. You need to be aware of this so you don't assume that because it is challenging for you, it is impossible. With a loving partner, self-awareness, and positive intentions, you can break through the tendency to be passive and become more expressive in your relationships. Don't get discouraged and defeated when it's awkward at first to explore the idea of your voice.

The next strategy is to practice. You don't want to get stuck overthinking these ideas. Your anxiety can talk you out of trying new pathways. Instead of just being the listener, engage in more dialogues. Practice sharing, opening up, confiding in those you care about. It's a good season to liberate your love life, so choose people who want to hear your voice. There are people who will want to know and hear from you. When you frame this as practice, it removes the pressure of believing you need to be perfect in your communication. Over time you can develop relationships that are based on truth and trust.

It's also necessary to develop resilience. Dear soul, I hope you will not be easily deflated by disagreement, criticism, rejection, or ridicule. Some people will prefer that you stay silent. Those are not the people of your soul's transcendence. They want you small, silenced, and easily manipulated. When you grow and embrace truth, some people will fall away. Let them. The true ones will remain or reveal themselves. Do not shrink. You have outgrown your former life. Those who love and care for you will celebrate your growth, evolution, homecoming, and breakthrough. Let the gift of authenticity and compassion be your North Star.

Ask yourself: Am I sharing the truth of who I am and what I think, feel, need, and desire, and am I sharing it compassionately? Am I creating space to hear the truth of my beloved, and is that space we are co-creating filled with compassion for them as well?

When you find it difficult to break the silence, attend to the healing of your inner child. Go back to the age and situation where you were silenced, and affirm that your voice has value. You matter, and so does your voice. Tenderly give yourself the message repeatedly that your thoughts, feelings, dreams, and needs matter. When you are silent and passive in your relationships, it leaves a gap. Something or someone is missing, and that someone is you. You have a unique contribution to make to your family, friendship, and romantic relationship. Be present for it. Your emotional, cognitive, spiritual, or vocal absence leaves any relationship incomplete. Show up in the wholeness of who you are.

Zaire grew up with clear messages from his family and peers that men shouldn't talk a lot. In his family, men would sit silently in front of the television drinking beer while his mom and sisters would have a lively chat in the kitchen. He learned from his father to see silence as a strength. He concluded unconsciously that silence was a symbol of endurance, toughness, and confidence. For some reason that he didn't understand, his partners would always complain about his silence. They could tell when something was bothering him, but he would never say what it was. Zaire finally realized that his father and some other men he looked up to were deeply dissatisfied. In his current relationship, he has started reflecting more and sharing with his partner what is on his mind. While it was initially uncomfortable, it was also a relief because it works. His fiancée is responsive and better understands what he feels and thinks, and he realizes there are some areas in which he has been making untrue assumptions about her in turn. Around his family of origin, he still goes into his silent mode, but in his relationship he has found the ability to open up.

ACTIVATION EXERCISE: Think of a relationship in which you feel most comfortable being your real, full, authentic self. Consider what about the person and your relationship has cultivated space for your assertive voice. Express gratitude to the person for co-creating that type of honest relationship. You can call, write, or express it in person. Be as specific as you can. The conversation can honor them and free you.

AFFIRMATION: I invite you to take a breath and place one hand on your throat. If it aligns with you, say these words: "There is power in my words. There is truth in my words. There is love in my words. I welcome my liberated voice so I can love more fully."

8

GENTLENESS: HEALING HARSHNESS AND RELEASING WARRIOR MODE

ello, gentle soul.

Yes, I'm talking to you. Even if you have had to fight your whole life, there is a gentle soul within you. As you tend to your heart, your gentleness will have more room to show up. I invite you to take a full, deep-hearted breath. To have a healthy relationship with yourself and others, you need gentleness. Gentleness is not weakness. Perhaps you grew up being told directly or indirectly that gentleness is for victims. The truth is, gentleness requires strength, especially in a world that can be so hard. Gentleness can be a psychological and spiritual resource. To invite ease, clarity, grounding, and breath in is to choose to nourish your heart. So I will say it again. Hello, gentle soul.

Gentleness is reflective of being at peace with yourself even when you don't agree with others. You can be at home within yourself so you are not easily agitated or offended simply because someone has a different opinion. Gentleness is not based in fear but in clarity about who you are. Are you clear enough about yourself that you don't have to convince others? You don't have to take up all the space and time in the room to convince people of your worth. You are not easily moved, provoked, or irritated. You are not a puppet. In your gentleness, you are a person with intentions, a voice. You are rooted, not reactive. You can breathe, speak, and act out of the gentle essence of who you are.

This is a good moment to reflect on the life experiences that hardened you. What and who led you to put up walls, disconnect from yourself and others, adopt a harshness to your tone and body language, arm yourself with vigilance, or permanently immerse yourself in warrior mode? If you think this is the way you have always been, perhaps the experience was very early in your life. It may have even begun with the prenatal stress that your mother had to carry. Other experiences that can lead you to harden are various forms of stress and trauma, including but not limited to poverty, family violence, community violence, oppression, sexual assault, harassment, incarceration, abandonment, and war. As you consider your experiences, appreciate yourself for all that you have survived. You got through it. It's helpful to realize that the ways you survived may not be the way you want to continue to live. While the harshness may have protected you, it has also cost you.

Being overly harsh can sabotage your relationships. It can lead others to avoid you, to be suspicious of you, not to be open with you, and to misread you and your intentions. Harshness can block your progress at work, hinder the development of romantic relationships, create barriers in friendships, and intensify divisions in your family life. Not only does harshness cost you relationally, but it also creates perpetual labor. Being harsh with everyone all the time is exhausting. You may have been doing it so long you don't even realize the energy and time it takes.

As you tend to your heart in this season, I hope you will consider laying down your armor. Give yourself permission, even if it is just for a moment, to release the tension in your body. You don't want to remain stuck in warrior mode. You are worthy of a life full of abundance and laughter. A full life includes gentleness in your body, heart, voice, and spirit. Precious, sacred one, there is a warrior within you, but there is more to you than combat. You have a fighter in you, but you are worthy of more than constant screaming, defending, surveilling, and fighting. This is an invitation for you to come home to yourself, and by that I mean for you to make room for softening, ease, gentleness. I know some of you may say, "That sounds appealing, but I don't even know how to be gentle." That's understandable. Perhaps you have never been taught it, never witnessed it, or never had the safety to explore it. The following are some strategies to empower you to embrace more gentleness.

CULTIVATING GENTLENESS: EMBODIED HEALING

Survivors of stress and trauma often hold their bodies tightly. You may have tension headaches, backaches, tense muscles, and a tight jaw. The rigidity in your body may also be reflected in the harshness of your voice and actions. To begin shifting into gentleness, you can start with your body.

Here is a guided relaxation exercise. After you read it or as you read it, explore what it feels like in your body. If you are comfortable trying it, begin by uncrossing your arms and legs, opening your hands as they rest on your lap, and breathing more slowly and intentionally. Starting with the top of your head and working your way down, tighten each part of your body and then release the tension, allowing yourself to feel the gentleness enter. As you tighten and release, you can say internally, "Warrior, release," or "I invite gentleness." Notice how your body and mind shift as you release the tension. Throughout the day you can check in with yourself and give yourself the reminder to release the tightness and embrace gentleness within your body and with yourself.

As you consider releasing stress from your body, gentleness also requires inviting breath into your body and spirit. Reconnect with yourself when you feel yourself drifting and disconnecting. This will remind you to soften. There is more to you than your roar and fire. There is more to you than fierceness and fight. As a trauma survivor and a psychologist who works primarily with trauma survivors, I know that distress often leads us to hold our breath. When you start breathing very shallowly, your nervous system reads the experience as danger. When we are in a panic because of perceived danger, we can become combative and escalate the tension around us. You may do this even in the presence of loved ones, especially if you have experienced harm by a loved one. I invite you in your present and future to be mindful of taking a breath before you speak to or storm away from your partner, children, or coworker. Take a breath and allow the harshness to melt. Take a breath until you embody a gentle, not a weak, spirit. Now you are ready to have a heart-led encounter.

CULTIVATING GENTLENESS: MINDFUL OF THE COMPANY YOU KEEP

If you are not harsh with everyone, consider in whose presence you soften. Ask yourself if you have constructed a life with people who are untrustworthy. If none of your friends make you feel at ease, you may have some challenging decisions to make. In other words, if your harshness is not because of your past but because you are currently in a toxic relationship or working at a toxic job, you may need to shift some things externally so that your gentle nature can emerge. If you have the kinds of "friends" or partners who are constantly belittling you, it will be hard for you to release any harshness.

To invite in gentleness, list the people with whom you feel safe, respected, comfortable, and at ease; to the extent possible, maximize your time with them. Select relationships and friendships that encourage gentleness over harshness. People who are safe to be around make your heart healthy and happy. You can breathe and just be in their presence. Consider also if people feel at ease in your presence. If you are bringing in the combat and warrior mode, it can also create a vicious cycle of distrust. Nourish your heart by choosing people who don't require constant warrior mode. Spend more time with people who allow you to let down your guard and embrace the gentle part of you.

CULTIVATE GENTLENESS: TAKING SACRED PAUSE

Harshness often emerges when we are triggered. In that state, you see everything and everyone as a threat. You may go into fight mode, where you are desperately needing to be seen, heard, and affirmed. Instead of being reactive and triggered, you get to choose how you respond. You don't have to perpetually unleash your inner warrior. To make this shift, you will need to slow down before you respond. Take time to breathe and reflect while asking yourself: *Is this reaction really about this moment or about some old scripts and wounds that this moment is somehow reminding me of?* As you take sacred pause, you also become mindful of your self-control and your own power. We speak and act harshly when we falsely believe we have no other options. I invite you to cut the strings of triggers and allow yourself to consider your options. It's a lie that the only thing you can do is escalate to a 10. There are infinite possibilities in every moment. Consider which of them align with the truth of you.

To motivate yourself to take sacred pause, remember the times you pressed send or post too soon, the times you said or did things you regret, and even the times you may have scared others and possibly yourself. When outrage is all that you feel, it can tell you false stories. Those false stories can damage your heart and the hearts of those you care about. With this in mind, consider the times and places you will take sacred pause going forward so you can speak and act in ways that align with your values.

CULTIVATE GENTLENESS: KNOW YOURSELF

Harshness can serve as a cover for the truth of what you really feel. By telling yourself the truth and addressing that truth, you can create space for gentleness and self-compassion. In your child-hood home or prior unhealthy relationship, it may have been un-acceptable to express how you truly feel. You may have covered those feelings with a harsh exterior. As you attend to your heart, get curious about what lies beneath your warrior mode. It may be fear, insecurity, or shame. As you learn to recognize the root of what you feel, your interior life can heal and grow. Tell yourself the truth about why you feel the need to fight everyone all the time. What is the story you are not acknowledging within yourself?

When you actively embrace the journey of acknowledging and healing the inner wounds, you will be liberated to expand your emotional life. You no longer have to operate based on one note—harshness. While toughness can be a part of you that you tap into when needed, if that is your permanent state, you are be-ing robbed of a full humanity. Choose to expand your interior life so you can show up with a greater range and depth, which includes gentleness.

I want to pause here for a cultural consideration. As a woman of African descent, I am aware that culturally some of us may show up with what appears to be a toughness even when we are not actually being hostile or aggressive. While I respect our cultural variations regarding emotional displays, I also invite you to consider within your culture those people you have encountered who have a gentleness or ease about themselves. It is a cultural myth that you must be in combat mode to be culturally authentic. Across cultures, there are people who model for us the strength of gentleness—those who can shed harshness in voice, action, and intention. Let's not conflate cultural authenticity with harshness. You can fully embrace your culture and simultaneously not perpetually battle everyone. Embrace your full humanity and the humanity of your community. You're worthy of all of that.

Last year, I had an opportunity to interview a group of Black women activists who have dedicated their lives to advocating for Black healing and liberation. While people may see only their toughness in protesting week after week, in rain, cold, or heat, facing online and in-person harassment and constant threats, I appreciated their sharing that they start most of their meetings with a meditation, creating space for their hearts, minds, bodies, and spirits to be nourished. One of the leaders who is a mother also shared that she was amazed by her young son, who when the police would not allow him to use the bathroom during a protest rally, sat in the street, closed his eyes, and began to meditate. She was heartened that she had taken the time to help her child develop his interior life so he was not reduced even in the face of adultification and erasure. While combative, oppressive times may cause the warrior in you to rise, I hope there is also room and safety for you to be gentle with your heart and the hearts of those you love.

As you work to transform or expand your heart for gentleness, be patient with yourself. Attending to your heart involves unlearning and deprogramming the messages that taught you that constant harshness was the only path for survival. You are in the process of reprogramming and learning the strength and gift of gentleness with yourself and others. Loudness and harshness are not always strength. The loudest, meanest voice in the room is not necessarily the strongest person in the room. Sometimes your old patterns will show up and you may choose the familiar triggered response of warfare. Give yourself permission to shift when you notice yourself slipping into old dynamics. Reflect on what motivated your prior programming and remind yourself of the why and how to show up differently. Also take responsibility for and, when appropriate, apologize for your harshness with your loved ones. You are on a journey of self-discovery. Let others meet your heart, not just your wounds. The old way is limiting. Having room for gentleness will open up new possibilities in your loving relationships.

CULTIVATE GENTLENESS: CARE FOR YOURSELF AND OTHERS

When you care about how your words and actions land on others, the impact of your presence, you will shape your relationships with compassion. In this way, gentleness will come into your partnering, parenting, work life, and friendships. Your care for yourself will shape the pace and rhythm of your life. Give yourself permission to shed the lie that you don't care. When you don't care about someone's feelings, you will say whatever you want with a harshness in both tone and content. When I care about you, I care about how you feel and the way you experience our relationship. I give thought to how I treat you and the way I speak to you. I also give thought to how I treat and think about myself. The truth sets you free. Sometimes our harshness reveals a lack of care for others. If you truly feel hate, disdain, disgust, and animosity for your partner or friend, you should ask yourself why you are choosing to be in this relationship or friendship. Sure, there will be moments of strong emotion and disappointment, but if that is the constant state of your feelings toward this person, you may need to look at how to heal this relationship or how to exit this relationship in accord with your values and truth.

Ask yourself, *Is there any gentleness in my loving?* If my loving is all about control and dictating and criticism, it is a limited love that may not be love at all. If my way of showing care is just to be harsh with the person I care about, it is time for me learn a fuller script. There are many ways to love. Telling people what to do, even our own children, is not the only way to show care. I invite you to consider the other ways you have felt cared for and the other ways you have expressed care.

CULTIVATING GENTLENESS: LOOK BEYOND THE SURFACE

It is helpful for us to see the fullness of people's humanity, not just their mistakes, errors, or shortcomings. If your teenager comes out of their room with a negative look on their face, instead of taking it as a personal rejection and yelling at them, you may get them to share more about what is going on in their world by using gentleness. If your friend seems to be irritable, instead of getting harsh with them, try gentleness; it may get them to share what is upsetting them. When you find yourself procrastinating, instead of letting your internal critic engage in constant trash talk and put-downs about yourself, treat yourself gently, with understanding and appreciation. Gentleness doesn't mean we avoid hard conversations or erase our boundaries or standards. It does mean that when we are addressing something, we are dealing with the root issue, not just the symptoms of distress. Real talk: We are complex beings. To have a healthy connection to ourselves and others, we need to have the audacity required to face the truth even when it's not pretty. Are you willing to see the truth about yourself and those you love? The truth may not be the first thing you see, but is the reality that persists as the various storms come and go. I hope you will look deeper and confront the deeper matters of the heart with radical revolutionary gentleness. In the midst of the trouble of the world, hold on to your spiritual, psychological gentleness, which is a way of holding on to yourself. Gently see your growth—in softening you can be more loving, more able to sustain relationships, more open to truth, and more limitless in your loving.

> *Linh grew up in a tough neighborhood. Although she has always been petite, she gained the respect of others with her quick wit, her sharp tongue, and the ability to launch rapid-fire insults and jokes about anyone who tried to challenge her. Linh's younger siblings looked up to her and were protected by the mere fact that others knew they were related to Linh. This gift served her well in her neighborhood and school, especially since her parents were immigrants and had difficulty speaking English. Linh was the family advocate and was praised for it. The challenge is that lioness Linh often had difficulty in love relationships. People who were attracted to her would either be men who wanted her to be their advocate warrior while she remained feeling unsupported or unprotected, or men who initially liked her but then resented her harshness and tendency to*

hide behind humor or the creation of what many of them called "drama." In counseling, Linh began to explore the false dichotomy she has created between being fiery all the time and being a weak woman who ends up victimized. She began to explore the nuance and range of her emotions and expressions, realizing there are times when her fire is necessary and times when it hinders the connection she authentically desires. Linh is much more selective about when she unleashes her inner lioness and is learning to enjoy the ease that comes with not having to fight all the time.

ACTIVATION EXERCISE: Apologize to someone you care about whom you have spoken to or treated in a harsh manner. It may have been a long time ago, but they will likely remember it, and this action can be transformative for the relationship when you can acknowledge the impact of your choices and your desire to choose differently going forward. If there is no one you feel the desire to apologize to, choose one to three ways to show someone you care with gentleness, not harshness. Speak kindly to them and do a random act of kindness that you believe will be appreciated by them.

AFFIRMATION: If it aligns with you, wrap your arms around yourself and simply think along with your breath—inhale gentleness, exhale harshness.

9

RELATIONSHIP BELIEFS: SHIFTING YOUR MINDSET

Ellen is a Jewish woman in her twenties. She was raised with the idea that the wife is the peacemaker of the home. The way she has interpreted this in her dating is the belief that she shouldn't voice complaints or too many needs and that it is her responsibility to make a relationship work. This has contributed to her staying in relationships despite her unhappiness with them, just in the hopes of being married. Even though she is only twenty-eight, she feels like she's getting old and is afraid of being alone.

I am so glad that you are on this journey of healing your relationship with yourself and others. One of the important tasks of healing your relationship with others is shifting your mindset about relationships from assuming negative outcomes to opening your heart to the possibility of positive outcomes. When you assume negative outcomes, you may avoid relationships or abandon yourself with the hopes of attracting and maintaining "love." Freeing your heart to receive and give love also requires transforming mindsets that may be limiting your experiences with love, whether romantic, friendship, or family.

There are different approaches to therapy, and I integrate several of them in my practice. These approaches include behavioral therapy, humanist therapy, feminist therapy, and liberation therapy. For this chapter, I want to focus on cognitive therapy. Cognitive therapy recognizes the connections between our thoughts, emotions, and behaviors. The relationship between the three is called a cognitive triangle. Here is one example to demonstrate how our thinking can lead us to take different paths. If you haven't heard from your partner all day even though you texted them "Good morning!" as soon as you woke up, you could come to different conclusions. One thought is that they are not interested in you, they don't respect you, or even that they are cheating on you. This thought may lead you to feel angry, rejected, and insecure. Based on those feelings, you may choose to act by leaving them a profanity-filled voice mail, not accepting their calls when they reach out, or spending your day crying and anticipating a breakup. On the other hand, you may think they must be having a stressful day, and as a result you feel compassion, concern, and maybe even worry. Due to those feelings, you may choose to send a message to encourage them, offer your help, or give them a warm greeting when they reach out. As you read this scenario, you may have assumed one response is right based on your lived experience. The reality is that both thoughts could be true. The person may no longer be interested or the person may have a lot on their plate today. You want to be mindful if based on past experience or observation of others' experiences, you always assume the worst. This can lead you to leave prematurely, to have difficulty trusting, and to never have the experience of working through tension to gain greater connection and clarity.

In this chapter, I invite you to identify any negative beliefs you have about relationships, the reason you adopted these beliefs, the costs of maintaining these beliefs, and finally the possibility of shifting these beliefs to thoughts that are more true, affirming, and healthy.

UNHEALTHY RELATIONSHIP BELIEF: LOVING SOMEONE WILL JUST RESULT IN GETTING HURT

If you read the section title and thought *Absolutely!* this is a belief that is likely affecting the way you feel about relationships and the way you act in relationship to others. You may feel a lot of anxiety, distrust, hesitation, dread, and insecurity. As a result, you may avoid relationships; consistently pick people who aren't available; remain distant, cold, and closed off; or even select partners who are mean and hurtful from the beginning.

Dyani is a Native American woman in her thirties who escaped an abusive marriage several times. On multiple occasions after being physically assaulted she ran away to her parents, but her father always made her go back to her husband. The final time she fled, she stayed on the streets until she eventually was placed at a shelter. When she began therapy with me, she was in transitional housing and had begun dating occasionally. Dyani shared her philosophy with me by saying, "Dr. Thema, I don't like those guys who act nice. They're just trying to trick me and catch me by surprise when they start hurting me. I'd rather go with a guy who is tough from the beginning. At least then, he's being honest and I know what I'm getting."

Dyani is assuming all men will mistreat her, and this belief is then shaping how she feels and how she chooses her next partner. What are the assumptions you make about harmful behaviors?

Once I had two students in my graduate psychology program get into a debate about infidelity. One student was a Christian and expressed her dismay that someone could make a vow to her and to God and then break it by cheating. Another student spoke up and insulted the first student by saying she was being naive if she expected faithfulness. The second student maintained that monogamy is impossible to maintain over time and that all people cheat. She believed that as long as there was no emotional connection with the outside person, infidelity was acceptable. In other words, for her, an emotional betrayal, not a sexual act, was the problem. Consider in this moment what you believe relationships will lead to for you. Which actions would be hurtful to you, and which do you expect or accept? How did you come to these beliefs?

Equating love with hurt can cause you to avoid intimacy. I invite you to broaden and add nuance to your ideas about love. While at times in loving another, you may experience disappointment, frustration, and, yes, hurt, there is more to love than those things. Looking at love more fully is what causes many people to keep showing up for it. Has the possibility of being hurt or disappointed overshadowed the gifts and beauty that comes with love? Instead of overgeneralizing that hurtful experiences are all that love has to offer, reflect on as the possibility of fulfilling, albeit imperfect, loving relationships.

UNHEALTHY RELATIONSHIP BELIEF: IT'S MY JOB TO FIX OR CONTROL MY PARTNER

Exerting control and manipulation over your partner is harmful to both of you. The assumption that you know best, that you are better, more evolved, more perfect, and your partner is less than you is an unhealthy framework that will create an unhealthy relationship. This approach has at its roots a lack of acceptance. Instead of choosing, appreciating, and loving people for who they are, you select people based on what you can make them become. While all of us need to grow and change, there is imbalance when the assumption is made that one person has all the growing to do and the other person is already fully evolved into their best self. The lack of humility and the arrogance, condescension, and pressure can create frustration, disappointment, and a sense of hopelessness for both partners. Instead of dreaming about who a person could be after they make a bunch of changes, think: *Can I love and accept this person as is? Can we grow together instead of my directing their growth?* In humility, are there things you can learn from your partner? Things you can learn from this relationship? Consider that if this person is unacceptable to you, perhaps they would be better loved by someone else and you could better love someone who is more aligned with your values or the characteristics you are looking for.

Linda is an African American woman in her late twenties. She has advanced degrees, and her fiancé does not. They both have above-average incomes. Linda came to see me about her anxiety, and one of the issues she was anxious about is her fiancé's unwillingness to read a set of premarital books she purchased. She had various ideas about what it meant that he wasn't reading the books. Most of these ideas led her to doubt his commitment to her and their future marriage. As we explored the issue, I asked her if in all the time she has known him he has ever been a reader. She said he is not. He prefers exercising, going out in nature, and watching films. We talked about how it may not be fair to judge his commitment to her by the number of books he is willing to read. As we explored possibilities in her individual sessions and she spoke with him, she discovered he was open to premarital counseling and to watching videos about marriage. If Linda had continued to try to turn her fiancé into a lover of literature, they might not have gotten married. She considered what she really wanted in a partner and gave herself permission to look at all of the ways he demonstrated his care for her and their future, as opposed to making the measure of his love one action that has never been a part of who he is.

I invite you to release yourself from the role of being your partner's therapist or parent. This may be a good place to take a breath. You can be a loving, supportive partner without being controlling. Actually, being controlling makes you less loving and supportive. If you are in a relationship or if this applies to a relative or friend, you may want to ask them in what ways they have felt accepted by you and if there are any ways they feel you are trying to force them to change. Some of you may be thinking: *But my partner needs to change.* If this is the case, it will be necessary for *them* to find their motivation for change—for example, engaging in healthier behaviors. Trying to force an unwilling person to change can do more harm than good. You can encourage them and ask how you can best support their desire for change. You can avoid behaviors that enable their unhealthy habits, but this should not be rooted in shame, control, or manipulation. Acceptance doesn't mean you have to like everything they are doing. It means you accept that this is where they are, and you get to make choices about how you want to engage with them based on this being where they are.

A deeper level of your healing will entail your asking yourself why you are drawn to people you believe need to be rescued, fixed, or parented. What do you imagine it would be like for you to be partnered or friends with someone who you saw as a peer? Do you wonder what would make them choose you or stay with you? Do you select projects instead of partners because their dependence on you, financially or emotionally, makes you feel more needed, powerful, secure? You may want to consider the story you have told yourself that labels certain people as off-limits or undesirable.

> *Monique is a forty-year-old Black woman who is highly successful. She has a history of dating unemployed and underemployed men who expect her to take care of them and fund their financially risky dreams. Each time, in the end, it turns out the men have cheated on her and set her back financially. Instead of working on her relationship skills within the relationships, we need to back up to the point of the selection process in order to determine what is leading her to believe that (1) her options are scarce and (2) men who need her will be more likely to commit to her.*

I invite you to release the myths and fears that have led you to be with people you don't like and give yourself permission to drop your control tactics and practice compassion, humility, and acceptance with the people you desire connection with.

UNHEALTHY RELATIONSHIP BELIEF: UNLESS I HAVE A PARTICULAR BODY TYPE, I WILL NOT BE DESIRABLE

Body shame and negative body image can create stress in relationships because they can dampen your desire for and comfort with physical intimacy. Any psychologist who identifies with feminist, body-positive, womanist, or social-justice-oriented psychology will tell you that these negative thoughts about your body did not just come from your mind. They may have come from earlier experiences with teasing, bullying, rejection, trauma, and ridicule. Not only have you had to deal with comments and actions from your family, friends, and former partners, but there is also the reality of social pressures, which present a narrow idea of beauty. This narrow window excludes people based on their race, gender, features, disability, age, height, and weight, among other characteristics.

Because of these messages from billboards to films to music videos to responses on dating sites, you may have insecurities about your body. As a result, you may not like for anyone to see your body, including your partner. You may not like your partner to touch certain areas of your body, because you are not pleased with them. This can lead to attempting to be intimate with someone while trying to hide yourself at the same time. Some of you cannot imagine making love with the lights on or without a shirt on. Some of you may also have difficulty with physical intimacy when you are sober. This may be a result of teasing and body shame, but it may also be related to trauma, whether in childhood, adulthood, or both. (If trauma is a part of your journey, therapy may be an important addition to your wellness practices.)

You may also find it difficult to accept compliments because you have such negative attitudes about your body. I invite you to begin to challenge these narrow ideas of beauty that are based in oppression and false hierarchies. It will be refreshing and empowering to begin to notice the beauty in yourself and others that does not fit these beauty myths. You may even want to give a gentle touch or massage to the parts of your body that you or others have rejected. Think and even speak loving words of acceptance to your body temple. Your body has been with you over the years, and even if there are things about it you would like to enhance or change, I encourage you to consider that you and your body are worthy of love, respect, and pleasure in your current state. The next time your loved one gives you a compliment, consider simply saying *thank you* instead of putting yourself down. The next time your partner reaches out to embrace you and the negative internal critique shows up in your thoughts, change the script by saying to yourself: *I give myself permission to enjoy this touch, this moment, and this love.* In addition, as you learn to accept and even celebrate your body, you may begin to be more free in your expression of your sensuality and sexuality. In other words, the journey is not just about being more receptive to your partner's looks or touches, but also about your being liberated to initiate and express intimacy as well. When you are not stuck in your head criticizing yourself, you open yourself to playfulness, joy, delight, and passion. Passion is not just for the people the world has decided are models, cover girls, or leading ladies or men. People of your race, gender, age, body size, disability, religion, and financial status are worthy of passionate love, too!

UNHEALTHY RELATIONSHIP BELIEF: ALL RELATIONSHIPS ARE HARD, SO IT'S BETTER TO STICK WITH WHAT I HAVE NOW

When we convince ourselves that good love, healthy love, mature love, or fulfilling love either doesn't exist or doesn't exist for us, we cling to unhealthy, dysfunctional, and sometimes even abusive relationships. We need to consider that we are worthy of being treated well, even if we have never experienced this before. You are worthy of good love. You may believe you're disqualified from good treatment because you have never received it. Perhaps family, fake friends, former partners, or even strangers have made comments that made you doubt that you are lovable. Or perhaps everyone you know who is in a relationship is miserable, so you have come to believe that is the way it's supposed to be.

> *Faith is a woman in her thirties. Her partner, Geoff, is in his forties. Every week, Faith describes how miserable she is in her relationship. Geoff constantly veers between ignoring her and putting her down, both in private and in public. The relationship is not satisfying at all, but Faith's fear that she wouldn't be able to find someone who would treat her better keeps her in it. She shares her complaints with her partner, but he either shuts down or begins to complain about her appearance and cooking.*

As you consider your belief that all relationships are difficult, consider the difference between a relationship's being work and a relationship's being abusive or unhealthy. Relationships are work in the sense that you and your partner are different people and have to learn each other's preferences, communication styles, personalities, values, and so forth. Compromise can be challenging, as it goes against our assumptions that people should think, feel, and act like us. Relationships can also be work when you face life's challenges: from parenting to financial stress to the loss of a parent to the development of an illness or a health condition. The key is when difficulty comes, you want to turn *toward* each other, not away from each other. So acquainting yourselves with each other and facing challenges with grace are where the work comes in. On the other hand, if the source of stress is not an external challenge but the actions of your partner—speech or behavior that demeans, belittles, humiliates, neglects, or mistreats you—then we are talking about an unhealthy dynamic.

Before you decide to endure, persist, or persevere, ask yourself, *Is this about our learning each other, facing external sources of stress, or one being mistreated by the other?* Once you have your answer, consider if this is an issue for you to work on together, if you want to seek outside support, or if you simply want to go your separate ways. Some people simply count the years they have been together as a marker of accomplishment without considering the health of the relationship. Long-lasting love can be beautiful—and you want to consider whether the relationship is rooted in love and respect or convenience and insecurity. Yes, you may want to read that again.

Give yourself grace and compassion to wonder, *If I believed people could treat one another well and build loving relationships, what would I decide to do regarding my current relationship?* In cases where it is mutual work, you may choose to engage in that work because the relationship is worth it. In cases where you are being harmed or you are harming others, this may be the time to consider making a different choice—one that honors you, the person, and the truth.

RELATIONSHIP UNHEALTHY BELIEF: IF MY RELATIONSHIP ENDS, I'M A FAILURE

Many people falsely believe that staying in a relationship is a good thing to do even when the relationship is killing you physically, emotionally, or spiritually. This belief, which is sometimes based in cultural or religious teachings, can result in your experiencing shame, embarrassment, and humiliation after a breakup or divorce. You may see yourself as damaged, inferior, unworthy, or unlovable. I invite you to consider whether some endings are necessary for your survival and growth. Has the feeling of being a failure or having family, friends, or strangers treat you like a failure in love affected the way you approach relationships? Maybe you have given up on love because you think you're not any good at it. Maybe you have avoided commitment because you fear "another failure." Perhaps you are defensive and always have one foot out the door as you emotionally prepare yourself for the inevitable end. These beliefs, feelings, and actions can sabotage your love life. I invite you to give yourself grace and compassion.

Let me offer you an alternative perspective. A relationship can fail without the individuals involved in it being failures. The ending of a relationship, including marriage, is an event, not an identity. Perhaps the relationship was good for a while or perhaps it was never a healthy relationship. Sometimes an ending can be a success. Leaving, releasing, and letting go may be markers of growth and psychological breakthrough. If you find that hard to believe, you may sign up for dating experiences that do not honor you because of the shame you carry. Shed the false belief that your past experiences in love have the final say on your identity and your capabilities. Shed that false belief that you are stuck, so you can be open to healthy love. Even if there are mistakes you have made in the past, consider owning them while not letting them own you.

Rewrite your love story—the story you tell about yourself in love. Reflect on how you might end these sentences using Tina Lifford's framing "Up until now but from this point forward":

Up until now, I have been emotionally distant in relationships, but from this point forward I . . .

Up until now, I have not been faithful or honest in relationships, but from this point forward I . . .

Up until now, I have not spoken up to express my needs in relationships, but from this point forward, I . . .

Up until now, I have _____ in relationships, but from this point forward I will

_____

Give yourself permission to write a new love story. Start with challenging and shifting your thoughts, opening your heart to a fresh experience, and engaging with others in healthy ways. As you heal your mind, you can heal your relationships. By creating integrity and consistency between your inner world and your outer world, you begin to live and love from a place of truth.

Miriam was married for over twenty years. She met her husband in college. He was a heavy drinker then, but so was everyone in their circle of friends, so she assumed he would mature out of it as others did. Unfortunately, he did not. She felt it was her duty to cover for him in front of their children, clean up after him on the nights he vomited, make excuses for him at social events, and be silent about his destructive behavior. After all that she endured, Miriam was devastated to discover her husband had a long-term girlfriend and another child whom he spent time with regularly. Miriam came to counseling after her divorce and felt great shame for having "failed" at love. We explored the ways she had been supportive of her husband and children and began to think about how her same traits and behaviors would look quite different in a relationship with someone who was not actively abusing substances. She began to see her strengths and with the encouragement of a friend went on a dating app. Miriam is excited about the person she has been dating for nine months. Her children are happy to see her happy and more confident in herself.

ACTIVATION EXERCISE: Select the belief that most connected with you and journal about the roots of the belief, how it has protected you, how it has cost you, and how you want to shift to healthier beliefs.

AFFIRMATION: If it aligns with you, place one hand on your heart and affirm that "Healthy, nourishing, respectful love is possible for me."

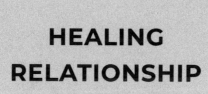

III.

HEALING
RELATIONSHIP
WOUNDS

10

HEALING PARENTAL WOUNDS AND ATTACHMENT ISSUES

Emanuel is an Afro-Latino single gay man in his thirties. His parents migrated to the United States to make a better life. When he was three years old, for reasons never explained to him, his parents took his older siblings and he was left with an aunt and uncle who made it clear that they did not want him. They did not treat him with the same care as their children, his cousins. After five years, he was dropped off one day at another uncle's home. His uncle was very quiet and struggled with alcohol addiction. He had various girlfriends and they were usually kind to Emanuel. He wasn't sure if their kindness was genuine or simply a way to gain favor with his uncle. At seventeen his parents sent a ticket for Emanuel to join the family in the United States. He feels disconnected from them and insecure and struggles with anxiety in his friendships and dating, but thinks that as a man, he cannot ask for reassurance. The feeling of needing anyone makes him uncomfortable, so potential dating partners often feel he is emotionally unavailable and sends a lot of mixed signals.

Some of us are carrying relational wounds from childhood. If you had parents or caregivers who were neglectful or abusive, whether physically or emotionally, it established an early script that may have carried over into your adult friendships and romantic relationships. These attachment issues can show up as anxiety, insecurity, or ambivalence. Regardless of what kind of upbringing you experienced, the good news is that it's possible to heal your heart and show up in the world in healthier ways. In this chapter, we'll talk about the individual work of healing, as well as the part of healing that can be done only in relationship with other people.

As I begin this chapter, I'm conscious of the fact that the kinds of parental wounds that readers may be carrying can vary widely in their form and depth. Some of you may have experienced physical violence and abuse; others may have experienced sexual violence and molestation. Some of you experienced emotional, verbal, or psychological abuse from the very people who should have been affirming, supporting, and nourishing you. Still others were neglected. Rather than physical assaults on your body or verbal daggers, you may have experienced silence and absence. In some cases, a parent may have been physically present but emotionally absent, while others experienced physical abandonment and lacked loving guidance and direction.

One challenge of having been wounded by a family member is that it often happened or started at a young age, before you were able to develop a sense of self in a safe and affirming environment. Some people may have even experienced abuse prenatally because their parents were struggling with alcohol or other addictions.

Those of you who are familiar with my work know that I often refer to the idea of homecoming, or being at home within yourself. I want to express appreciation for those of you who are opening yourself to this healing journey even though the home you've experienced hasn't always been a safe, loving, or healthy place. I am grateful for your willingness to take the risk of creating a place of flourishing, freedom, and unconditional love that you may never have experienced before. Thank you for joining me, even if you never had a real, consistent, or reliable sense of home. While it is painful to confront past wounds, it's also empowering to know that we can give ourselves what our parents either couldn't or wouldn't give us.

While you may have grown up in a place of shame, fear, insecurity, instability, or danger, that place is not your home. You can create within yourself a home that is not at all like the home you survived or escaped. Even as I say that, I am mindful that some of you may still be living in a difficult environment for various reasons. In a toxic environment, you may have had to disconnect, dissociate, separate your mind from your body, or tuck parts of yourself away. Being at home within yourself means gathering the broken, scattered pieces and creating a sacred home within yourself where you feel psychologically, spiritually, and emotionally safe.

BREATHE AND PROCESS
YOUR EMOTIONS

I am going to outline four key aspects of healing parental wounds, the first of which is breathing and being present with yourself and your feelings. It can be incredibly painful to confront past wounds, so I encourage you to take care of yourself and go at your own pace—pause and come back if you need to. You may want to invite a friend into your healing process for extra support.

If you grew up in an emotionally or otherwise abusive home, you likely had to stay outwardly focused much of the time, constantly monitoring other people's moods. Some of you couldn't experience a peaceful night's sleep because you had to stay vigilant even then, so it is a radical act of self-affirmation to give yourself permission to breathe.

As you breathe with intention, you come home to your breath and your body. You're no longer stuck in your head, trying to analyze what everyone else is doing, ruminating over your behavior, or coming up with a plan. As you sit still with your breath, you can tell yourself truths you may not have been able to express aloud. Some of you grew up in homes where you couldn't say what you truly felt, thought, or needed—perhaps because you would be disrespected or attacked, or you wouldn't be believed. Others grew up with emotionally fragile parents who couldn't handle the truth of your life experiences, so even as children, you felt like you had to take care of your parents and carry the weight of your experiences and emotions alone. As a result, you learned to lock away your feelings and needs, not requiring anything of anyone. For those of you who have spent a lifetime emotionally bound, your healing process involves breathing and recognizing that you don't have to be strong all the time; you can care deeply and feel deeply because your experiences matter. Buried within, you may find a broken heart and a flood of unshed tears, so healing requires getting in touch with all those feelings that you may never have had the space to share with anyone, much less experience for yourself.

In addition to grieving past experiences—perhaps for the first time—some of us are mourning the childhood we never had. You may feel sadness, depression, or even despair that you have never acknowledged because you kept yourself busy or disconnected to avoid confronting the pain. I want you to know that your tears are welcome here. If you've kept your grief locked away for years, it may feel unimaginable to let your pain rise to the surface, so again, I invite you to take your time, go at your own pace, and honor what you feel you need to express in this moment, even if it's just a wordless moan.

In addition to feeling grief and despair, some of you may experience anger and rage, because what you went through was outrageous. You may have grown up in an environment where it was unacceptable for you to express anger, even if horrible things were said or done to you. If you feel overwhelmed at the prospect of confronting all these emotions, I encourage you to pay attention to your body, your mind, and your spirit. If they are telling you that you can't or don't want to do this by yourself, consider seeking therapy. While you may have family and friends you can turn to, a skilled professional can help you walk through the process of getting in touch with previously unacknowledged or unexpressed parts of your pain.

Give yourself permission to feel what you feel, breathe, and tell yourself the truth. How do you really feel about your parents and what you experienced? Are you resentful? Do you have questions that you don't think will ever be answered? Are you depressed or anxious because you never allowed yourself to take in the magnitude of what happened? Are you worried about how your relationships with your parents or your feelings about yourself might change once you acknowledge the magnitude of what happened? You may want to journal your responses to these questions. There is healing in the truth-telling process, even if you're only acknowledging those truths to yourself and no one else. Learning to be at home within ourselves means making the decision to stop deceiving ourselves and start honoring the truth as we see it, regardless of whether we receive other people's validation, approval, or support. We are embarking on the healing process for the sake of the child we may have had to leave behind in order to survive.

Processing our emotions and experiences with the people closest to us can be complicated. You might even think, *You don't know, Dr. Thema, that I was a bad kid, so that's why my parents had to do what they did.* Although this may have been the message you received and internalized growing up, I want you to know that when a child is acting out, this must be addressed, but it is not a justification for verbal, physical, or sexual violence or abandonment. When we reflect on our early years, we sometimes judge our childhood selves by adult standards. But as an adult, you would make different choices than you did at age eleven. So we breathe and give our childhood selves permission to make mistakes and not know some things that we have since learned. The moments when we made mistakes as children were opportunities for our parents and guardians to show up with love and care to nourish and guide us, but they may have failed to do so.

Breathe in the complicated layers of feelings you may have about yourself, your parents, and your childhood. As you breathe, give yourself permission to release the tension that you may be holding in your neck, your forehead, the base of your back, or the pit of your stomach.

BUILD YOUR IDENTITY

The next step in healing parental wounds is building ourselves back up in the aftermath. Some of us are living with the ongoing reality of our parents' disapproval or verbal or emotional assaults on our psyches, but we refuse to allow ourselves to be defined by those who seek to destroy us or are not emotionally equipped to honor, love, or care for us. As we remake ourselves from scratch, we may want to take some of the ingredients that we learned or developed from our families while leaving others behind; my recipe is not going to be identical to that of someone who sought to dismantle or erase me.

The field of womanist psychology emphasizes the importance of defining ourselves. For those of us who have lived our whole lives holding our breath, waiting for the approval of those who don't even approve of themselves, I encourage you to claim your agency, recognizing that the fact that someone has said something about you doesn't make what they said true. You don't have to hold on to others' false definitions of you. What did your parents say about you? What aspects of this resonate as true to you? Is anything they said about you untrue? Did they say something or treat you in a way that made you feel less than, unqualified, unworthy, dishonorable, shameful, dirty, or insignificant? However you were seen or treated, you do not have to internalize that version of yourself.

We refuse to define ourselves by the words or actions of people who never really saw us. After breathing and connecting to what we feel, we transmute those emotions into the act of self-definition. We refuse to remain stuck in grief, anger, bitterness, or resentment. Rather, we alchemize those feelings into new definitions of ourselves. After grieving and feeling outraged by the wounds of our past, we take a breath and recognize that we are no longer in that place; we are here in the present moment.

Those things happened to me, but they are not me. I experienced what they said and did, but they do not define me. So who am I? I get to decide.

Some of you may feel grief and frustration that you are defining yourself for the first time later in life. Perhaps you wish you had been able to develop that identity as a child. You cannot change the past, but you can take this sacred opportunity to reclaim your pen, take it out of the hands of your guardians, and write your own story. Create your own narrative, name, and identity, because, after all, you are rebuilding yourself.

SET BOUNDARIES

Another key aspect of healing parental wounds is setting boundaries. We each have to reflect on our specific circumstances and decide: *At what level can I interact with people who are still trying to dismantle me?*

Your parent may have experienced some kind of transformation. Perhaps they are now sober, or they are going to therapy, or they're repentant about past actions. Although it may be difficult for you to trust this new behavior because of your upbringing, you can see them changing. Even as you see these improvements, boundaries are still necessary as you and your parent learn about each other in this new dynamic.

On the other hand, perhaps your parents exhibit the exact same mindset and behavior as when you were a child. If your parents continue to reject, condemn, erase, or control you, then it is essential for your health and wellness that you set boundaries. I cannot dictate what those boundaries should look like, because you have to take into account your personal needs and circumstances, including cultural, religious, and financial considerations. All I can tell you is that your wellness is essential, but it is very difficult to be well if you spend a lot of time with people who don't care about your well-being. How can you rebuild your self-esteem if you're always around people who tear you down?

Some of you may decide that you don't want to deal with your parents at all. Others of you aren't going to cut off your parents entirely but are going to spend less time with them than before. Still others of you may be living with your parents for various reasons, so you're going to have to come up with strategies to emotionally and spiritually fortify yourself so the verbal arrows do not land. Boundaries don't have to look like physical separation; you may have emotional or spiritual boundaries, but not a physical one. However your boundaries are set, the goal is to not be dismantled by others' opinions of you.

As you consider what you want your boundaries to look like, I'd like to reiterate that boundaries are going to look different for each person and family. So don't you go telling your mother that Dr. Thema told you not to talk to her anymore. That is *not* what I'm saying. As an adult, you have to decide on your boundaries for yourself and own your decisions. I encourage you to take your time and search your heart when it comes to figuring out what kinds of boundaries will help you flourish. Some examples may include (1) setting a time limit for your visits, (2) noting that you will leave if certain behaviors are engaged in and then following through on that statement, or (3) not allowing certain members of the family access to your children.

BUILD THE BRIDGE TO YOUR FUTURE

Finally, healing parental wounds involves creating a bridge to your future. Some of us may be stuck waiting for our parents to finally parent us so that we can move forward with our lives. If this resonates with you, it's time to build a bridge over your parents' inadequacies so that you can walk confidently into your future.

If you feel like your life has stagnated because you have been waiting for your parents' love, approval, or guidance, or because you've been grieving the childhood you never had, I have difficult but empowering news for you. Some of your parents will *never* be able to give you what you wanted or needed. This means that you can create psychological, emotional, and spiritual medicine for your inner child by parenting, loving, and nourishing yourself. You can find a community that respects and loves you. Regardless of your parents' shortcomings, you can find healing individually and in community so that you can step into your purpose, your gifts, and your calling. Your life is not doomed because of your parents. Your life does not end with their judgments, ignorance, rejection, or own unhealed wounds.

Instead of trying to figure out what went wrong or why your

parents weren't able to provide what you needed, acknowledge and grieve the childhood you never had, and then take your life into your own hands. You no longer have to wait for your parents to be who you wanted or needed them to be. Your life, your authentic life, is calling and waiting for you. You don't have stay stuck in the quicksand of disappointment over your early years. In this moment, time, and place, know that there is a new you waiting on the other side of that bridge. Leave behind what you choose to and gather the pieces you want to hold on to; then walk across that bridge and into your homecoming.

IDENTIFY YOUR ATTACHMENT STYLE

One aspect of building a bridge over your parents' inadequacies involves addressing any attachment issues you might have as a result of your upbringing. Attachment refers to our capacity to connect emotionally with other people. There is a great body of research exploring how the attachment styles we experienced from our caregivers in childhood can shape our attachment style and relationship patterns in adulthood. When we better understand our roots and early life story, we can gain clarity about how we operate in friendships and romantic relationships. As we heal, we develop healthier approaches to dealing with others. The inner work we're doing should be evidenced in our capacity and willingness to connect with other people with compassion and respect.

As we go over the four main attachment styles, I invite you to reflect on your upbringing. How reliable were your parents, guardians, or whoever raised you? Could you depend on them? How nurturing and loving were they? Did you feel seen, heard, understood, and valued in their presence? Or did you feel erased, uncertain, or dismissed when you were around them?

A healthy attachment style is secure. This doesn't mean that relationships are perfect, but they're nourishing. When I am secure, I trust other people's good intentions toward me, and I know that I am worthy of care, attention, love, and respect. If I grew up with a secure attachment style, I felt that there were people who authentically and sincerely cared about me and my thoughts, feelings, and needs. From this strong foundation, I feel empowered to explore my identity, form relationships, and investigate the wider world and its possibilities. I am able to take healthy risks with my career and dive into love because I believe that love is possible for me. If I have a secure foundation from childhood, I find it easier to navigate relationships in adulthood because I feel secure within myself.

Another attachment style is anxious. The anxious attachment style is characterized by uncertainty. This means that in a relationship, I feel uncertain about whether I can really trust the other person. I am uncertain about whether they truly see and care about me. I am uncertain about my own value and significance. In a moment of conflict, I might be uncertain about whether the other person will come back. If I feel insecure, I constantly need friends and romantic partners to assure me that they care about me, but no matter what they say, it's never quite enough. No matter how many times they show up for me, I don't quite trust it, so this relationship pattern is filled with worry, dread, insecurity, and anxiety.

The third attachment style is avoidant. Avoidant people also experience uncertainty, but unlike anxious types, they respond to that uncertainty by shutting down rather than seeking affirmation. If I am avoidant, I am likely very good at cutting people off if I see the slightest sign that they might not care about me. I avoid connection and intimacy and make myself emotionally unavailable because I don't want to get hurt. I tend to reject other people before they can reject me.

Both the anxious and avoidant types are insecure, but they respond to their insecurity in different ways. People with an anxious style need attention and assurance, while avoidant types feel threatened and pull away as other people get to know them better. If you are anxious and gravitate to someone who's avoidant, it can set you up for confusion and heartache unless each person does the necessary healing work around their attachment issues.

The last attachment style is disorganized. In both romantic and platonic relationships, disorganized types send mixed signals: it seems like they're all in, and then they're out, but then they're back in. This can leave you wondering, *Are they ghosting me, or am I their soulmate? Which is it?* This shaky foundation makes it difficult for disorganized types to ground themselves in a relationship, to invest themselves in it, and develop intimacy over a sustained period of time.

While challenging, it's possible for all of us to heal our attachment issues.

CLARIFY YOUR STORY

The first step to healing is clarifying your story, which means truly knowing yourself. You cannot heal what you do not acknowledge. Our relationship issues are not about having bad luck picking people. We need to recognize patterns when it comes to those we're drawn to and what feels comfortable and familiar to us. We ask ourselves: *What do I tend to ignore? What sends me running in the other direction?* When we see ourselves clearly in terms of how we show up in relationships of all kinds, we can then ask the question: *Why is this so?*

Some of us disconnected from ourselves because of trauma or neglect. Those experiences might have trained us to go into survival mode, which continues to affect how we respond to other people, how intimacy makes us feel, and how we feel about our-selves. Whatever we experience in our internal world subse-quently shows up in our external world.

If our attachment traumas happened very early in life, we may think, *It's just me. That's just how I am with people.* But when we come home to ourselves, we recognize the truth of our stories and understand that we are more than our traumas and insecuri-ties. We aim to return to our authentic selves, those that existed before we were told that we were unworthy. Even if you can't re-member who you were before the rupture took place, or if your insecure attachment began when you were just a baby or even before you were born, you can still come home to yourself.

Healing begins with taking the risk of telling yourself the truth. What do you notice about the friends you choose? How do you act as a friend? How do you feel when you're in the presence of someone who really sees you? Do you see patterns in how you behave in romantic relationships? What fears affect your decision-making? How does fear affect your perception of things and the way you speak to other people? What fears, anxieties, and worries affect your attitude toward love, and how have you addressed those fears? What have you run from, and what have you run to-ward? Telling yourself the truth is the only path back to yourself. You have to see and understand the real you and the child you once were.

Recognizing our wounds is the first step to healing them. It's easy to point out everyone else's flaws, but it's harder to see our own issues. While we couldn't prevent our wounds from happen-ing, it is within our power to heal those wounds and carve out a new path for ourselves. This requires you to ask yourself if you truly want your relationships to change. Do you want to deepen your friendships? If you're happy with the way things are, you won't have room for growth. But those of us who desire healthier relationships and a deeper capacity to connect with other people have work to do. While our growth ultimately benefits us and everyone around us, it isn't easy. If you've been following the same patterns for years, it takes conscious effort to shift out of old habits, but you are worth the effort.

EVALUATE YOUR CURRENT ENVIRONMENT

Once you've clarified your story, it's time to examine your current environment. If you are surrounded by unsafe people, it's going to be difficult for you to heal your attachment issues. You can't be open, trusting, and vulnerable if you have a shady partner who disrespects you and friends who don't really care about you. In order to heal, it's vital to assess your current life and determine if it's safe.

First, we can figure out whether we are surrounded by untrustworthy or dangerous people. If so, we can strategize about how to shift our environment. Separating yourself from unsafe people may mean that you're on your own for the time being, but it's imperative to heal in a safe environment. We want to get to a place where we're around people who are trustworthy, as far as we can tell.

Post-traumatic stress disorder was first identified in veterans when they'd returned home from battle and were in the process of healing. So we have to ask ourselves: How can we heal if we're still in battle? In my therapy practice, it's a different experience if I am counseling a person who *used* to be in an abusive relationship, compared to counseling someone who is still with their abuser. The latter remains in survival mode, while the former can heal and move forward and thrive. We cannot be free if we're in a toxic space.

HEALING ATTACHMENT ISSUES

In addition to honestly assessing your environment and relationships, you must develop a sense of self. This goes back to building your identity in the aftermath of parental wounds, as was discussed earlier in this chapter. We cannot put our identity and worth in the hands of others, because if they drop us, we are left with nothing. On the other hand, when we have a strong sense of self, we don't lose ourselves even if we are hurt or disappointed by other people. In order to be in healthy relationship with other people, we need clarity about who we are and who we want to be; we accept and appreciate ourselves.

There has been some debate in the field of psychology about whether it's unfair to tell people to work on themselves before they can have a healthy relationship, because some healing can happen only in community and in connection with other people. True, there are both individual and communal aspects of healing. I can't sit here feeling like I'm nothing until someone tells me that I'm something, because that would mean I'm basing my whole identity on what they tell me that I am—that would be a false self. Instead, I want to develop some clarity within myself about who I am while also being open to supportive corrective experiences with other people. I also want to be intentional about those I consider friends and choose to share sacred space with.

I do not use the word *friend* lightly. Friendships, like romantic relationships, develop over time. I open myself up gradually, and in the process, I also observe the other person. I note how I feel in their presence, and I pay attention to how they respond to my vulnerability and imperfections. These observations tell me whether I should take a step forward or a step back in the relationship. A relationship doesn't have to be all or nothing, and it can evolve over time. I can't heal my attachment issues if I cut myself off from people entirely.

As you get clarity on who you are, and as you decide who to share your self, your space, and your time with, tune in to yourself. Over time, you will become more and more aware of your needs and your responses and reactions to other people. If you notice yourself retreating from someone who really sees you, it might be your old habits at work. But once you are aware of your story and your patterns, you can choose to shift away from fear, anxiety, and avoidance.

Think about who, if anyone, has been a real friend to you. What qualities and characteristics of that person stand out to you? And then I want you to think about whether you've been a true friend to someone else. What did it look and feel like to show up for that person? As we become more at home within ourselves, we can also make others feel at home in our presence.

Dana's mother struggled with addiction throughout Dana's childhood, and a result, Dana never felt loved or even viewed as a priority. When she lived with her mom, various men came into the house who were sexually abusive. Dana's mom either didn't believe her, blamed her, or ignored the abuse. She was often left home alone or dropped off with various relatives for weeks or even months before her mother came to pick her up. Dana learned not to depend on, trust, or believe others. Dana is now a mother of three in her late thirties. She is emotionally distant from her husband and children. Her love languages are gifts and time, but she has difficulty with verbal expression and physical affection. Dana came to therapy to break this cycle of disconnection. With behavioral therapy and therapeutic support, instead of waiting until she felt different, Dana committed to beginning to act different. Even when it felt uncomfortable or "weak," Dana began telling her family that she loved them and initiating hugs and affection. While they were at first confused and thought something must be wrong, her family has embraced the changes, and Dana feels good about beginning to break the cycle so her children will hopefully not grow up with the hyperindependence that she grew up with. While Dana acknowledges that some-times she says caring statements because she feels she is supposed to in order to be a good mother and wife, she also says there have been times when she has wanted to say them, felt them, and could enjoy them. Her most empowering moment, Dana says, was realizing she didn't have to be her mom. She could make a different choice. Dana wishes her mom would stay sober and go to therapy so she could one day get free, too.

ACTIVATION EXERCISE: Journal or share with a friend or therapist the way an early experience before you were twelve has affected the way you show up in friendships or dating relationships. Consider if this is a pattern that works for you or if there is anything about it you would like to change.

AFFIRMATION: If it aligns with you, say these words: "I am building my capacity to trust and love. I am growing more secure within myself and in my ability to make connec-tions with others."

11

LONELINESS

Maya is an African American single woman in her thirties. She has only ever had short-term romantic relationships. She is smart and successful, with a number of good friends. She is active in her community and church, often volunteering to help others. One of her favorite roles is being an aunt and a mentor. But she is lonely and grapples with the idea that she may never be married or become a mother, two roles she has looked forward to her whole life. She has tried various strategies to find a partner. She has had makeovers, from changing her style of dressing to her hair, with no real results besides some compliments by strangers who never follow up. She has gone to singles mixers where the majority of attendees have been other single women. She has tried dating sites where the men who approach her either quickly send sexually suggestive messages or continuously text small talk and never ask her for a date. Maya is a Christian and has also prayed a lot for God to send her a husband. She came to therapy thinking something must be wrong with her for her to still be single. Her many years as a single woman, along with the stigma and judgment from others, has chipped away at her confidence. She has a lot of love to give and hopes one day she will be able to express it.

THE DIFFERENCE BETWEEN SOLITUDE AND LONELINESS

Whether you are single or in a relationship, you may be struggling with loneliness. In this chapter, we'll talk about how to recognize and heal our loneliness. As we begin, it's key to understand the distinction between solitude and loneliness; just because you are alone doesn't necessarily mean that you are lonely. For example, you might be single and live by yourself but not feel lonely, spending some evenings alone and others engaged with your community, whether that's with your nieces and nephews, neighbors, or colleagues. On the other hand, if you don't feel comfortable in your own skin, you can never truly enjoy solitude because you feel disconnected from yourself. And even if you do enjoy solitude, you can still experience moments of loneliness. The truth is that we all feel lonely sometimes, and we all need connection with other people, so I invite you to release any shame you experience around your desire for connection.

DESTIGMATIZING LONELINESS

Some people speak in a derogatory way about those who share their experiences of loneliness, equating loneliness with a lack of self-love, but I want you to know that this is a faulty assumption. You may be working on yourself, you may have come a long way, you may even love yourself, but you can still feel lonely at times.

Loneliness can take different forms. You may feel like no one really knows you, gets you, or spends quality time with you, even if there are "friends" around. You can be dating or married and still feel lonely. You could be at a family reunion, surrounded by people to whom you are related, and still feel lonely. Loneliness is not just about a physical absence of people around you but about a lack of authentic emotional connection. We need to feel at home within ourselves in the presence of another—whether in the context of friendship, partnership, or familial relationship. It is normal and healthy to desire authentic relationship with others; this certainly does not automatically mean that you are needy or dependent or insecure.

There is something beautiful about being known and knowing another. There is something beautiful about friendships that withstand trials. There is something beautiful about intimacy and healthy companionship. So if you are feeling lonely, do not judge the loneliness. Do not condemn yourself for feeling lonely. Acknowledge any loneliness you might feel without shame. After all, loneliness is a universal experience.

Some people have experienced seasons when they were so hurt—perhaps in the midst of a breakup, separation, or divorce—that they didn't even feel lonely. They may have felt so dismantled by the ending of a friendship or a relationship that they wanted to spend the rest of their lives in isolation. In these cases, getting to the point of desiring connection again is far from a bad thing; it may even be an indication of growth and healing. So when they start to reawaken, when they feel they may begin to trust again, when they start to heal and develop greater self-awareness and insight into the lessons they learned during those difficult times, then they may see an awakening of their desire for connection, friendship, or romantic relationship. If you've been there, it is crucial to recognize where you are in the process.

START WITH SELF-AWARENESS AND HEALTHY RISK-TAKING

When we aren't aware of our own loneliness, we can make destructive decisions. Sometimes loneliness can blind us to the truth because we are so focused on our need and desire for companionship. What might this look like? It might mean I want a friend so badly I miss the warning signs that this person is not my friend, and I continue to cling to them because I want connection. The same thing can occur in the romantic arena. I might desire companionship so intensely that I ignore areas in the relationship where I feel unfulfilled or where I can't show up authentically. If I am in this person's presence because I just want someone present, I have to tell myself the truth and recognize my loneliness without letting it obscure my view of the truth.

As we address loneliness and isolation, I want to reiterate that I am not coming at it with the attitude of "You just need to love you." While self-love is significant, it does not preclude emotional pain or longing for a deeper relationship. If you are feeling lonely, I encourage you to find some things that you can do on your own. People who don't have close friends or a partner can easily end up self-isolating and doing nothing, so take the risk of doing things in your own company. That's one of the beautiful things about feeling at home in your own body.

Are you comfortable going out to eat by yourself, not just sitting in your car to eat during your lunch break? Are you comfortable going to the movies by yourself if there is a show that you really want to see and you don't have someone to go with? Are you willing to go to an art gallery, a religious service, or a concert by yourself?

Even as we acknowledge our need for connection and companionship, recognizing that these are beautiful things to desire and working to develop that aspect of our lives, we must refuse to put our lives on hold. Too many of us are waiting until we have a boyfriend or girlfriend, husband or wife, to start our lives; we are waiting for other people to bring us joy. But you can live a full life now. Don't wait until you have a boyfriend or a girlfriend to travel. As you develop deeper friendships over time, what are some ways that you can bring joy into your life in your current circumstances, so you're not just waiting for others? You can also consider what prior experiences have affected your confidence and comfort in interacting with others. For example, the pandemic, discrimination, and prior unhealthy connections may make you anxious or avoidant when it comes to socializing.

I invite you to intentionally find spaces where you can spend time around other people, even if they do not require a lot of interaction. Past hurts and social anxiety can make it difficult to form friendships and relationships, so it may be easier to self-isolate. Be gentle with yourself, taking one step at a time as you gradually become more comfortable with other people. Some social settings are less demanding than others and don't require you to engage with people on a deep level. For example, you could take a class on something you're interested in, whether it's cooking, practicing an instrument, or learning a new language. There won't be a lot of pressure to develop friendships in those spaces, but you'd meet people with similar interests, and simple interactions could potentially develop into authentic connection. You could join a book or hiking club, or a meditation or Bible study group, where you can experience spiritual growth in a community without a lot of social pressure. Think about things that you would enjoy doing in the company of others while putting minimal stress on yourself.

I personally enjoy spoken word. I love poetry, so I attend spoken word readings where people go up to the mic and share their poems. I can just sit there, listen, and clap. I can make small talk with one or two people, but there is no pressure to perform unless I want to get up and share one of my poems. The point is that I can start by taking smaller risks (simply showing up at events) and gradually get more comfortable in those spaces, engaging with others in deeper ways over time.

CULTIVATE THE RELATIONSHIPS YOU ALREADY HAVE

As we learn to connect with others, I invite you to consider the people who are already in your life. I have worked with clients who tell me that they don't have anyone, but as we continue to talk, they'll mention different people, and I'll have to ask, "Well, who is that? And who is that?"

It's easy to overlook what we have, so ask yourself: Do I want to improve the friendships that I already have? Or am I really starting from scratch? Do I actually have no one? Or are there people in my life with whom I wish I had a more substantial relationship?

Loneliness is sometimes rooted in fear and distrust. This is most commonly the case for people who are lonely even when they are surrounded by other people. Have you kept your friendships superficial? Or have you been hurt in the past, so it's become difficult for you to open up again? In a dating relationship, it's possible to experience physical intimacy without emotional intimacy, all the while saying that you want more. But true intimacy requires vulnerability.

You might be surprised to find that when you take the risk of being vulnerable and transparent, others are more likely to do the same. If you have a group of friends who just talk about fluff all the time, you might assume that no one in the group wants to have deeper conversations. But can I let you in on a secret? The others may be longing for more meaningful connection as well. So rather than making a false assumption, take the risk of venturing into deeper waters and being honest with people about how you feel.

Being vulnerable is especially valuable for those who are used to being the strong one in a relationship. If you hold on to that identity, you'll never really let people in. It's very lonely to always be the giver, and you may end up feeling resentful or disconnected from the same people you're trying to help.

It is necessary to cultivate spaces where you do not have to wear the mask of perfection, where you can speak freely about what is going on in your life rather than hide behind the automatic response "I'm fine. How are you?" Do you find yourself asking a million questions about someone else because you're trying to distract them from what's going on with you? If you do this, you can feel lonely. Which people would you be willing to risk vulnerability with and try having a deeper conversation with? When you think about your acquaintances, friends, and dating partners, with whom are you willing to share what's really on your mind, your needs, your past hurts, and your dreams for the future? What are the parts of your story that you consistently edit out and keep people from knowing about you? When might you be willing to go deeper?

Greater connection requires require greater vulnerability. Although vulnerability can feel scary, being really and truly known is worth the risk. This is what it means to be at home with yourself, not with a script or a mask, not as Superwoman or Superman, but as the real you in the company of another.

For those of you who are in dating relationships or marriages where you feel lonely, what would it mean for you to risk showing up for real, to stop going through the motions, to stop coexisting merely as roommates? To clarify, when I talk about showing up for real, I don't mean simply sitting someone down and sharing your list of grievances. That wouldn't truly require vulnerability on your part because you'd be putting all the blame for the problems in the relationship on the other person. What would it look like to show up with honesty, to openly share your desires and your wounds with the goal of repairing the relationship, instead of just venting?

Some of us are lonely because we haven't invested in the reparative work required in any relationship. If you've known someone long enough, conflict will arise at some point, so make sure to properly address ruptures. When you think about each of your friends, you have to decide: Am I willing to do the work of repairing this relationship? Is the other person also willing to invest in repair? Or is the relationship done? And if it's really over, am I still holding on to the relationship, clinging to someone with whom I don't feel safe, and keeping myself in this lonely place?

Once you've done this honest and thorough assessment of the relationship, you might find that you don't want to keep investing in it and you need something new.

HOW TO FIND YOUR PEOPLE

If you don't have a friend or partner that you can trust and who appreciates you for who you really are, you may need to get into new spaces to meet other people. How can you meet anyone new if you just go to work and return home every day and stay at home every weekend? Where are your people supposed to find you? We have to be willing to step outside of our comfort zones and our old routines. After all, there is a saying that insanity is doing the same thing over and over again and expecting different results.

If you spend all your time with people you don't enjoy, or stay at home by yourself but keep saying that you feel lonely and want connection—well, the old routine is not working for you. Unless the deliveryman turns out to be your soulmate, I don't know how you're going to meet anyone new. Wherever you live, I invite you to look online and find something that is happening in your city—whether it's a fair, a festival, a lecture series, or a concert.

I also recommend getting involved in an organization that reflects your interests. While it's great to go to one-off events, people don't often spend a lot of time talking to strangers. Rather, they stick with the people they showed up with and then leave with those same people. But if you join an organization or group that meets regularly, that usually creates more opportunity for conversation. In this context, you can observe other people, get a sense of them, and develop greater connection over time. You may have to get out of your comfort zone while working to build up those relationships.

Reflect on past friendships and dating relationships and the lessons you gleaned from them. If I don't have clarity about what damaged my past relationships, then I am likely to repeat the same mistakes and continue to have relationships that do not flourish. I'm not looking solely at what other people did to me, but also considering any role that I played in how I chose my friends, how I have treated them, and how I showed up in those relationships. What challenges do I experience around intimacy, whether on an emotional, a physical, or a spiritual level? In what ways, if any, have I sabotaged past relationships?

Someone recently wrote to me about owning their part, recognizing how they had ruined what could have been a good thing in their last relationship. We want to be honest with ourselves about how we may have sabotaged relationships, chosen or been attracted to people who were problematic, or closed ourselves off.

Nobody likes to be rejected, but if I'm always walking around looking unapproachable or angry, or if I seem arrogant or my attitude communicates that I don't want to be bothered, then I'm standing in my own way of connection. It is foremost to try to get a sense of what I may need to heal and grow so that I can be more open to connection.

As you begin the work of self-reflection and personal growth to enable you to develop more meaningful relationships, I'd like to recommend two last things that can help you on your journey. First, I encourage you to engage in volunteerism so that you can give back and be around other people as you act in service to others. After all, it's a blessing to bless others. Volunteering may also give you the opportunity to encounter kindred spirits who care about the same things you do—whether it's taking care of the environment, of abused children, or of animals. You can clean up public spaces, participate in political protests, or become an activist for the things that speak to your heart and spirit. As you open yourself to this process, you both give and receive.

Finally, I recommend moving your body and getting active. When we are lonely, it's easy to self-isolate, stay at home, and become couch potatoes, binge-watching the television and scrolling on our phones. All of that has an impact on us physically, emotionally, and spiritually, so despair and emotional pain get stuck in our bodies. The loneliness can eat us up. When we hold loneliness in our bodies, it affects the way we carry ourselves—the way we walk, talk, and communicate.

Kevin is a forty-four-year-old African American man. He is divorced and estranged from his siblings and parents. He works at a predominantly White company where racism is pervasive. He doesn't socialize with his coworkers and usually eats lunch

*at his desk, in his car, or at a nearby restaurant by himself.
Kevin works out but doesn't talk to anyone at the gym except
to respond to the person at the check-in desk. He occasionally
attends church online. He came to therapy complaining of depression, which he reports as being rooted in a deep loneliness.
We explored the conflicts that resulted in the end of his marriage and his disconnection from his family of origin. The story
he has told himself about love and connection is that they require perfection. He has come to believe that if he is not perfect,
people will abandon him, and that when others are imperfect,
he needs to cut them off so he doesn't get hurt further. In speaking it aloud, Kevin could see the problematic thinking that has
led him to sabotage the possibility of connection. To begin to
shift the direction of his life, Kevin has begun at least once a
week eating with a Black coworker in the cafeteria, going to
church in person (he's thinking about joining the choir), signing
up for a speed-dating event (with the short exchanges being
just long enough for him not to get too anxious), and the biggest step of all, making monthly calls to one of his siblings.
These steps are moderately stressful, but he's decided to "do it
afraid," knowing that the alternative is the deeply dissatisfying
isolated life he has created. His heart is opening.*

ACTIVATION EXERCISE: If you're at home right now and
this speaks to you, I invite you to put on a song about love
for family, friendship, or a romantic partner, get up, and
dance to release whatever you're carrying in your body. If
now is not a good time, I invite you to make some space
later today to put on some music, move, and breathe so
that you are not consumed by loneliness as you make the
commitment and take the steps to live fully and

authentically, honoring your connection with yourself and with others.

AFFIRMATION: If it aligns with you, read these words aloud: "I desire friendship, companionship, and connection. There is no shame in that. I honor my desire for deeper connection."

12

HEALING FROM INFIDELITY

Barbara is a White neurodiverse woman in her forties. She has three children and recently found out her husband has been cheating on her throughout the marriage. She contracted a sexually transmitted infection. When she confronted him about it, he did not deny it. Initially he said he was sorry, but as time went by, he began blaming her for it. He said she wasn't fun anymore. Barbara is shocked and disappointed. She is trying to decide if she should fight for the marriage or move on with her life. She can't imagine staying and also can't imagine being single again at this age and with three children.

Unfortunately, infidelity is common, which makes the topic of this chapter—healing yourself and your relationship in the aftermath of unfaithfulness—all the more weighty. I'm grateful to walk alongside you on your healing journey.

Infidelity can be traumatizing, disruptive, and heartbreaking. It can destroy your trust—in yourself and others—and bring you to a place of despair. Experiencing infidelity is a form of loss, grief, and trauma. In this chapter, I'll talk about how you as an individual can heal from infidelity, as well as how couples can reconnect and rebuild, restore, and sustain a relationship in the aftermath of infidelity—if that's what you choose to do. I want to emphasize that trying to save a relationship after experiencing this kind of betrayal is a choice people have to make for themselves. Chapter 15, which covers releasing someone who doesn't love you, may be helpful if you or your partner has decided to end the relationship.

This chapter focuses on those of you who are trying to remain in a relationship after infidelity, rebuild trust, and work on healing yourself and the partnership. Let's pause and take a cleansing breath before we begin. I also invite you to go through this chapter at your own pace.

FEEL THE FULL SPECTRUM OF YOUR EMOTIONS

Being cheated on can be a totally overwhelming, upsetting, and devastating experience. It can break your confidence—not only in the relationship but in yourself. For some people, the infidelity came as a complete shock. Others may have experienced growing suspicion over time. And for still others, the cheating may have been blatant and in-your-face, so these people could be processing many different layers of emotions.

The first thing I'd encourage you to do is to feel your feelings. Give yourself permission to feel the full spectrum of your emotions, whatever they may be. In order to survive, or perhaps because they are in shock, some victims of infidelity respond with the attitude of, "I don't care." They may create a wall to try to protect themselves. Sometimes people keep themselves busy or distracted—with work or other people's lives or any number of things—so they don't have to confront the pain. I encourage you to make space for yourself and the fullness of your emotions.

While it can feel scary to open the floodgates, acknowledging and expressing what you're really feeling is essential for your healing. You don't have to succumb to the pressure to pretend to be fine or unbothered by what's happened. Be free to feel your emotions, in whatever form they appear over time.

You may be in shock because you never thought your partner would do something like this. Or if they've cheated before and assured you that it would never happen again, you may feel another wave of devastation, something like "I thought I knew you" or "I thought I knew where we were at." You may feel intense rage, anger, frustration, and irritation on multiple counts—because of how you were betrayed or what your relationship was like beforehand, for example. Of course, each person's experience is different, and the form the betrayal takes runs the gamut.

Some of you may have thought your relationship or marriage was fine or even good, so the discovery of infidelity feels all the more shocking, leaving you wondering, *What in the world happened?* And then there are those of you who already found the relationship unfulfilling, or perhaps you felt disrespected on multiple levels, and so infidelity feels like the icing on the cake or another item in a long list of grievances.

Some of you may be experiencing fear, wondering if your partner will leave you for the other person. You may be anxious about sexually transmitted diseases. You may be grappling with the question of what this means for you, especially if this was the person you'd thought you were going to do life with. When that boat gets rocked, you may be left wondering: Is this still my person? What will my future look like? How will this affect our children? How will this affect me financially? How will this affect my health?

And then there's the fear of other people's opinions. You may be asking: Who else knows? What exactly do they know? Whose side are they on? You may be experiencing a sense of panic around these questions.

Some of you are in a situation where you know the other person involved in the infidelity, so you may be experiencing fear about whether you can trust not only your partner but also the other person, whom you may have considered a friend or a trusted family member, a colleague, or a member of your church. You may be experiencing immense anxiety and stress around who, if anyone, is truly trustworthy. If you are someone whose faith is central to how you see yourself and how you make sense of the world, you may have questions and doubts. Where was God in all of this? How could something like this happen to someone who's trying to be a good person?

There is research that shows that heartache is not only emotionally painful but can also show up as physical pain in the body. When you are distressed, you may experience physical symptoms like body aches, backaches, teeth grinding, insomnia, picking at or losing your hair, picking at your skin, and skin breakouts, among others.

Some of you may be experiencing depression. Perhaps you are having difficulty feeling motivated, or you're feeling stuck, both emotionally and physically, so it's hard to get out of bed. You may find it hard to concentrate, and things that you used to enjoy now feel meaningless.

Perhaps you are experiencing confusion about what to do and how to feel because this is not how you thought things would turn out. This is not the kind of relationship that you thought you would be in. Your partner is not the person you thought they were.

In the midst of all these whirling thoughts and feelings, doubts and questions, give yourself permission and space to grieve. You may be grieving the loss of what you used to have or of what you thought you had. Some people may be thinking, *Oh, what we had was so good, and then things turned sour.* Others may learn that the relationship was never what they thought it was. So whether you are grieving what used to be or what never was, give yourself space to experience the fullness of your grief.

DON'T RUSH THE PROCESS

You are a human being whose emotions matter. They matter whether or not the other person apologized. Sometimes people think an apology is a magic bullet that will solve all their problems. The perpetrator may think, *Well, I apologized, so you should just get over it.* But betrayal hurts on such a deep level that it takes time to process and work through your emotions. Reminders of past hurt may appear further down the road and bring the grief flooding back, so please be patient with yourself.

If you and your partner are trying to stay together and rebuild the relationship, your partner will need to be patient with your process. Trust can be broken in an instant, but it takes much more time than that to be restored. You may experience pressure from your religious community or even from yourself to forgive and move on quickly. You may tell yourself, *I'm over it; let's just move forward*, while still struggling emotionally, physically, and spiritually.

As you take the time you need to heal, I encourage you not to make any quick decisions. The experience of infidelity can turn your world upside down, so feeling confused is natural. You may not know what you want to do. Do you want to believe your partner? *Should* you believe your partner? Do you want to rebuild the relationship? And if so, what would that mean for you and your future? These are really big questions, so I invite you to extend grace and compassion to yourself and give yourself the gift of time—time to be still, to get centered, and to gain clarity about the reality of your situation, which may be very different from the fantasy that you had hoped for. What is the present state of your relationship? Can you see and hear clearly when it comes to where the other person is in the relationship? What is the truth? What is a possible path forward?

You need time and space to reflect on these questions, and this will look different for every person. Some may need time away from their partner to clear their head, while others may feel that if they get away, they're never going to want to come back, so they'd rather stay together and try to work it out. People have done it both ways, and you are the only expert on yourself. So take the time to reflect and be honest with yourself, focusing not on what your partner wants or what you think others in your community want, but on what you need.

Try not to send your partner mixed messages. Say what you want. Sometimes people say they want space when they actually want their partner to fight for them. Or they tell their partner, "Let's just move forward together," when they really need space. You understandably may be confused about your own desires, so if you thought you wanted one thing but realize you want something different, communicate those shifts to your partner. You may tell them, "I know I said I needed that, but this is where I'm at now." Keep the lines of communication open as you take time to process your experience.

FIND YOUR SUPPORT SYSTEM

It is especially valuable when you're experiencing the upheaval of infidelity that you have the support you need, but be selective about those you confide in. Some people don't want to tell others about experiencing infidelity because they're worried others may think less of them if they decide to stay with their partner. Those reactions depend on the kind of friends and family you have. You want a support system that will be there for you regardless of where you land. You don't want people who are going to try to make decisions for you or dictate your actions. Rather, you want people who say, "I want the best for you. I want you to be treated well. I want you to feel loved, and I want you to know that you are deserving of love. So if that means staying in this relationship, I'm here for it. And if that means ending the relationship, I'm here for it."

Don't suffer in silence. When you're brokenhearted, your perspective can become clouded and you may need a sounding board. Sometimes you just need the release of saying something aloud rather than hiding in the shame of "I'm embarrassed and don't want people to know because it could mean something negative about me." Sometimes people keep infidelity a secret because they want to protect the unfaithful partner, but it is unfair to prioritize their wellness while you are suffering alone.

Confiding in others becomes a problem if those people feel like they have the right to make decisions for you. I also wouldn't recommend running around and indiscriminately telling people about something so personal, so be thoughtful about those you trust with this information. If you're spiritual, you may want to prayerfully ponder who to confide in, who would be a safe space for you, and who would want only goodness in your life, whatever that may look like.

Whether or not you have a family member or friend like that, I also recommend therapy as a safe place for you to process what you're thinking and feeling, to ask yourself the question: *Where am I in all of this?* Therapy gives you the space to grieve and start to figure out your way forward, the path that's best for you personally and for both of you as a couple. Be intentional about finding the right community and therapy for you. Support groups can also be useful; hearing from people who have had similar experiences can provide perspective.

You may have friends who have experienced infidelity, because unfortunately it is so common. I just want to caution you to remember that you and your friend are not identical. Sometimes people who have gone through similar things want you to handle it exactly the way they did, but that may not be the best path for you. It's helpful to know that you're not alone, to recognize that many others have been in this same place, so keep checking in with yourself and acknowledging the similarities between what you and your friend or relative have experienced while also understanding that you and your relationship are unique. Reflect on how their path can help you on your path, as well as on how your paths may be different.

MINIMIZE THE COLLATERAL DAMAGE

I encourage you not to seek revenge. If you've experienced betrayal, then your first thought might be *Well, they did it to me, so I'm gonna go out and have sex, too. Then we'll be even.* That logic may seem to make sense when you're in a state of hurt and panic, but seeking revenge is emotionally destructive whether you're trying to move forward on your own or as a couple. It creates an added layer of complication to work through in your healing process, especially if you're trying to rebuild the relationship. If the revenge sex has already happened, know that you will need to do additional work individually and collectively in order to move forward.

Get back to the basics when it comes to taking care of yourself; don't neglect yourself. When people are in a place of complete devastation, they may lose their appetite or their ability to sleep or focus. They may stop doing things for themselves, and as a result, they may feel an even greater sense of disconnection. Their heart may feel hard, or they may be checked out because they're so overwhelmed, or they might just be tearful all the time.

Ask yourself some basic questions: Did I eat today? Do I need to drink some water or hot tea? If I normally take vitamins, did I take my vitamins today? Can I stretch or move my body?

Since we hold stress and grief in our bodies, it is helpful to move, walk, dance, cycle, or do yoga or other exercise to release the tension. This is what we mean by embodied healing. Be careful not to turn to overeating, substance abuse, or anything else that may feel comforting in the moment but will ultimately make you worse off. These unhealthy practices can create a vicious cycle of turning to something for relief that ends up adding to your sense of despair.

Try to get on a regular sleep schedule even if you have trouble falling asleep. Spend some time lying down, letting your body rest even if your mind is racing. If your mind feels blank, give your body permission to be still.

If you have children, it is crucial not to involve them in the details of what's happening to whatever extent possible. Some people rely on their children for emotional support, treating them like a therapist or a best friend, but no child should feel the pressure of being responsible for their parents' mental health. It is also unfair to make your children feel like they have to pick a side—choose someone to be loyal to and someone to reject. We don't want to put that weight on our children.

It's one thing if your partner has done things that directly hurt their ability to parent, but it's also possible for there to be problems in your relationship with your partner that don't involve the children at all. Some people may justify oversharing with their kids by saying, "Oh, I'm just being honest, and they have a right to know." Well, it's really crucial to determine what's age appropriate for your children to hear, as well as what your true motivations are for sharing these things with them. Be careful that you're really prioritizing your children's needs rather than your own when it comes to what you tell them.

On a practical level, get tested for sexually transmitted diseases and infections. While no one wants to think about STDs, I encourage you to take care of your health. Both you and your partner should get a full medical screening so you can figure out whether anything else needs to be done.

DEALING WITH ALL THE WHYS

In the aftermath of infidelity, resist the urge to blame yourself for other people's choices. Each individual is responsible for how they choose to show up in a relationship or marriage. Some people are up-front and honest in admitting that they didn't have major complaints about their marriage or relationship, but they were still unfaithful. To be clear, I'm referring to people who were deceptive about being with other people, as opposed to being in a previously agreed-upon open relationship. When we talk about unfaithfulness, we're talking about people who lie and aren't following through with what they agreed on or vowed to do.

Some victims of infidelity experience inner turmoil while comparing themselves with the person with whom their partner cheated, especially if the victim knows or has seen that person. You might feel like you're not beautiful enough or exciting enough, or just generally not enough. I want you to know that you are deserving of love, care, and respect. You deserve to be pursued, wanted, and desired. Resist the urge to beat yourself up, and be intentional about rebuilding your self-esteem and sense of self-worth in the aftermath of infidelity.

It is necessary for the person who was unfaithful to sit with their reasons for doing it. Oftentimes the reason isn't complicated, which can be dissatisfying to the person who was cheated on. The unfaithful person may have just wanted more. They might say something like "Our relationship has been fine, but this was something different, which made it exciting." Perhaps the affair was exciting simply because it was unrelated to household responsibilities and obligations.

As a result of gender socialization, some people were raised with the idea that all men cheat. I have male clients who say they don't have a single male friend who doesn't cheat; that's just what everyone does, so that's their reason for being unfaithful. They have the attitude of *Why not?*, which of course can be upsetting for their partner to hear. Needless to say, women and gender-nonconforming people can be unfaithful as well. However, some people grow up hearing that it is acceptable for some people to cheat but not others, often based on their gender.

Nevertheless, it's important to get at the root of whatever is going on with your partner so you know how to move forward. If you hope to stay together and you don't want them to cheat again, you have to understand the mindset that led them to cheat in the first place. In order for your partner to modify their behavior, they have to shift their thinking. They may also need to do some perspective-taking, because often there was no thought of their partner when they decided to cheat.

If your partner is unfaithful and not self-reflective, you may be trying to pull an answer out of them as to why they cheated. Often it's not that they are unwilling to tell you but that they just haven't given it much thought. They might say, "I just did it," or "It was just available." In situations like this, especially in the immediate aftermath, the person hasn't done the internal work to give you an in-depth answer.

But as we think about the journey forward, it's going to be valuable for you and your partner to process what happened. Both couples therapy and individual therapy can be helpful. Some people who have been cheated on will want to know the full story of what went down. Others will say, "I don't want the details. They'll just play over and over again in my head." But some people will need more information in order to move forward, in which case the unfaithful partner will need to answer their questions if they're trying to rebuild the relationship. If the straying partner refuses to answer, it may make the other person feel like the unfaithful one is still lying or can't be trusted. They might not know how to move forward without that information, so communication is key.

REBUILDING A RELATIONSHIP
AFTER INFIDELITY

When you are trying to rebuild the relationship, there may be a need for greater accountability. If you've been unfaithful, your partner may want to check in with you more often because they may panic when they don't hear from you, wondering, "Where are you? How do I know that's *really* where you are? How can I trust you?"

If you feel like you're being surveilled, try to understand where your partner is coming from rather than responding with something like "I apologized, so stop watching me." If you're in the process of rebuilding trust that has been broken, your partner's need to check in more frequently makes sense. So if you're sorry for what you did, try accommodating your partner's needs rather than acting like a victim who's being harassed now that you have to answer more questions and call more frequently. Your infidelity has led to these circumstances, so accept the consequences of the broken trust.

This also means not trying to fix the relationship with sex. Some people think, *Oh, it was just about sex, so if I make the sex more exciting now, we'll be all better.* Healing a relationship is a holistic process, so while sexual intimacy is part of that, and infidelity can make it more difficult for people to reengage in that aspect of the relationship, you also need to prioritize emotional fulfillment and participate in deep conversation and quality time with your partner. Engage in all these aspects of the relationship without denying what has happened.

Finally, try to create some new and beautiful memories with your partner. If the last thing you experienced was the disruption of infidelity, then it may be hard to see a reason to move forward as a couple. Nourish the relationship by doing things that you enjoy together. Remind yourselves why you liked each other in the first place. What was it that made you fall in love with this person? Is that person—or at least a part of that person—still there? Rebuilding the relationship involves reconnecting and in some ways rediscovering the other person so that you have the inspiration and motivation to work through the difficult parts of the process. You and your partner both have to believe that the relationship is worth fighting for.

Mark has been unfaithful in all his dating relationships and in his marriage. He reports that the infidelity is not from a lack of love or satisfaction with his marriage. He has always thought of infidelity as the norm. He doesn't know a single married man who has not cheated. Prior to his wife's finding out, he thought about it as harmless fun. The women always knew he was married and were accepting of the circumstances. Now that he is in danger of losing his marriage, he is desperate to regain his wife's trust but acknowledges he also needs to build trust in himself. He is not sure he can be faithful because he's never tried. He is afraid of letting himself and his wife down again. We explored why he wants to remain married, why he wants to be faithful, and what activities end up being pathways to infidelity. He committed to closing these doors to unfaithfulness, including not going to certain places, not hanging out with specific male friends with whom he usually spends time finding other women, cutting off communication with the women he has cheated with, changing his gym, which is primarily a social club, and not asking new women for their contact information. He also committed to reopening doors with his wife. Instead of coming home and isolating himself in his man cave, he spends time talking with his wife, initiating affection and affirmation, and restarting their weekly date nights. The road ahead feels long for both of them, but Mark loves his wife and is working to rebuild trust and connection.

I'm sorry if infidelity is part of your story, but I'm glad that we could walk through this difficult chapter together. Whether you are now single or in the process of trying to rebuild the relationship, know that I extend my best wishes to you. If you are the person who was unfaithful, getting caught and trying to figure out what's next can be devastating for you, too. I want you to know that I'm very aware of the challenges you are facing.

My hope for all of us is that we get to a place of wholeness, wellness, and truth, and that we can discover what it means to really love other people and ourselves, not only with our words but also with our actions.

ACTIVATION EXERCISE: Have a conversation with a friend about what you should do now instead of focusing more time on why the infidelity happened. Begin to explore the possibilities of what you would like to do at this stage of your life.

AFFIRMATION: If it aligns with you, place your hands on your heart and whisper quietly, "My heart is worthy of care, love, and respect. My heart is worthy of healing and wholeness."

13

REPAIRING BROKEN FRIENDSHIPS

Seneca and Jennifer have been friends for over a decade. They were childhood friends and are now in their late twenties. The rupture in their friendship came when Jennifer was mistreated by a mutual friend. She expected Seneca to sever the connection with this person as she had done. Seneca remained cordial and at times friendly with this person. Jennifer was surprised and hurt by this "betrayal" and stopped communicating with Seneca. They had to make a decision to allow the friendship to continue to drift apart and die or to try to revive it with truth and difficult decisions.

Although ruptures in friendships can be incredibly painful, they're rarely discussed. This chapter addresses a couple of problems that often crop up between friends, in addition to offering guidance on responding to conflict with directness and maturity. Rather than simply cutting off someone who might have been a good friend or staying silent and remaining upset with them in an unhealthy dynamic, you can learn the essential skill of conflict resolution.

In this chapter, we'll talk about what to do if you or your friend is jealous of the other. I'll also cover a common dynamic in which one friend always seems to be the "strong one" in the relationship. If your friend is extremely capable and resilient, it's easy to overlook signs that they might be just as overwhelmed as you are. By recognizing these signs, you can learn to be a better friend and avoid potential resentment. Finally, we'll go over the steps to take in the aftermath of a conflict.

SIGNS OF JEALOUSY

Not only is jealousy common, but it can be extremely destructive in a relationship, so we want to be aware of signs of jealousy between friends. Some people will just come right out and tell you. If they're particularly self-aware and direct, they might say, "I'm so jealous"—whether of your life in general or a specific aspect of your life.

Jealousy is about desiring something that you don't have but someone else does. Simply wanting something that your friend has isn't necessarily wrong or unhealthy, and it doesn't make you a bad friend. Perhaps someone else makes friends easily and has a lot of them, while you are shy and marvel at how comfortable they are interacting with new people. You might feel jealous that they don't experience the same level of social anxiety that you do. Or maybe you are struggling financially while your friend has a high-paying job. You might experience jealousy around the fact that they don't have to stress about bills the way you do. Or suppose that your friend has a loving partner or spouse, and you hope to have a caring relationship like theirs. Or maybe you are experiencing fertility issues while all your friends have children. Recognizing your own desire or need is not toxic or unhealthy, but jealousy can show up in harmful ways depending on what you do with your unmet needs and desires—both within yourself and in how you respond to others.

You'll be able to recognize that your friend's jealousy is a problem if it prevents them from being able to celebrate your good news because they feel too frustrated, bitter, or disappointed that they don't have what you have. If you have to censor your good news because your joy makes your friend miserable, this can be a problem—it's not a real friendship if your happiness bothers the other person. If you start to notice that other people are angry, negative, or dismissive when you share about a blessing, or if they make backhanded comments and hide insults in humor—they're smiling or laughing, but you recognize the sting in their words— these are warning signs that their unmet need or desire is polluting the relationship.

Another sign that the jealousy has become toxic is if your friend is constantly trying to compete with you. If you mention something you've accomplished, they might feel the need to outdo you or draw the attention back to themselves. People who are secure in themselves don't constantly require all the praise and shine; they can sit with your story without making it about them. Friends don't compete with friends—it's not that kind of party. We want everyone in the friendship to win. My desire for my friends is for their dreams to come true. I deeply and authentically want my friends to feel happy and fulfilled, to prosper and thrive in their purpose.

Competition is different from having friends who motivate you. If you see your friend take a leap of faith and reach their goal, it might inspire you to pursue your own dreams. Think through whether your friends are a source of motivation—you're like iron sharpening iron, making each other better simply by being in each other's presence—or whether you are trying to one-up each other.

Another sign of jealousy is if your friend tries to make you feel bad about yourself. This person might believe that you have too many good things, so they try to bring you down and insult you, perhaps calling it constructive criticism when in reality it is just meanness. Of course, real friends can give each other feedback, correction, guidance, or insight, but the tone in which it is delivered is central. Is it coming from a place of love, or is this person really trying to break your spirit? Are the words rooted in anger and hatred?

If you are consistently leaving your friend's presence feeling that you've been attacked or like you have to walk on eggshells, this is a sign that jealousy or other issues related to insecurities and self-esteem are poisoning the relationship. The other person has moved from simply desiring more for their lives to perhaps trying to block opportunities for you. As the saying goes, "With friends like these, who needs enemies?" You can learn a lot about the depth of a friendship by the way people talk about you when you're not there or whether they remain silent in spaces where other people are speaking negatively about you.

Again, wishing that you had something that you see in the lives of your friends is not a bad thing in and of itself. It just means that you are not where you want to be, that some of your friends may be further along on the journey. The unmet desire becomes problematic if your unfulfilled dreams cause you to mistreat or compete with your friend or prevent you from being supportive and happy for them. We must recognize those distinctions in ourselves and others.

WHAT WE CAN AND CAN'T DO ABOUT JEALOUSY

Friends who experience jealousy fall into two categories. The first group may not have what you have, but it is within the realm of possibility for them to attain it. They can actively work toward that aspiration. For example, if they haven't graduated from college but you have, they might recognize that if they direct their focus, time, and resources toward that goal, it is well within their reach. A lot of my friends like to write, so if one of us has never published anything, that person might do some research on how to make it happen. They can go after that dream without getting negative or putting down others who have already achieved it. If my friend is in a loving relationship with her partner while I'm in an unhealthy relationship, observing my friend's relationship might prompt me to ask central questions like: Do I need to end my own relationship? Do we need to go to couples counseling? What needs to shift in my life for me to be in a better position to receive the love that I desire? In these cases, jealousy is easier to address because there is something you can do about it.

The second category consists of people who are jealous about something beyond their control. Perhaps it's related to some attribute they were born with or the family they were born into. I have a friend who is short and has always wished she had long legs. You, too, might lack a physical characteristic that you desire or that society celebrates; maybe you wish that you had a feature like your friend's. If this is the case, try to be aware of the things that you desire but that aren't in the cards for you and to show yourself compassion while refraining from putting down your friends.

Holidays like Mother's Day and Father's Day can be difficult for people who have a fraught relationship with these family members. While you can choose the relationships you have with friends and mentors, some aspects of your life are baked in, and it's imperative not to hold it against people who have better relationships with their families. You can grieve an absence in your life without making your friends feel bad about having what you don't. This requires self-awareness and emotional maturity. If you catch yourself feeling resentful, be intentional about shifting your thoughts so you don't sabotage the relationship.

Friends should support and celebrate each other. It's important to step outside of ourselves so we aren't always centering our own thoughts and emotions at the expense of the feelings and perspectives of others.

NIPPING JEALOUSY IN THE BUD OR TAKING A STEP BACK

If you think your friend might be jealous of you and it hasn't gotten to a super problematic place, you may want to talk to your friend about any negative words or actions they directed toward you without saying that they are jealous. Whatever your friend's motivations may be, it's up to them to wrestle with why they said or did what they did. You could simply say, "You are my friend. When I shared my good news with you, it seemed like you were upset about it. That doesn't feel good to me as your friend because it makes me not want to share things with you." Your friend might not even realize how they were coming off or how it was affecting you, so it's essential to name your feelings. This creates the opportunity to shift the friendship in a positive direction.

It might also be helpful to give your friend a more realistic picture of your life. Sometimes we get jealous because we think someone else has the perfect life, that they have everything they could possibly want without a worry in the world. We tend to center the things we don't have and lose sight of the greater context, thinking, *Oh, if I only had that, I would be so happy.* Someone with fertility issues might be jealous of someone else who just had a child, without realizing her friend had had three miscarriages prior to that. We often don't know the entirety of other people's stories. You might be jealous of someone who has a well-paying job without realizing that they experience panic attacks as a result of the pressures that come along with the role. It is especially key in a friendship to see each other as full human beings, which requires some level of transparency, vulnerability, and sharing.

It's also vital to acknowledge and celebrate your friends' achievements and strengths, because people often overlook what they're good at and focus on their perceived weaknesses. You might think that your friend has a lot going for her, but she does not recognize her own gifts, so it can be encouraging to remind her of these things. We often don't see the value of the things that come easily to us. I have a friend who's great at baking, but when I bring it up, she seems startled. She grew up baking, and her mother and grandmother were bakers, too, so it doesn't seem like a big deal or worth mentioning. Sometimes it's helpful to let your friends know what you admire and appreciate about them.

Finally, make sure that no one friend is dominating the room, that each person has equal opportunity to share their hopes, dreams, and disappointments. It's beautiful to walk with loved ones through difficult seasons, times when they may be struggling with disappointment, but they shouldn't be taking it out on their friends. If you try to encourage your friend but all you get back is negativity, if you celebrate them but they never celebrate you, or if you leave room for them in the conversation but they're always trying to talk over you, then you might consider whether you want to take a step back. If time spent with your friend usually makes you feel worse, this relationship might be one you don't want to maintain. Work to give your friend gentle feedback so they have an opportunity to shift the dynamic, but if nothing changes and you constantly feel uncared for, as if you have to tiptoe around them, I recommend that you at least reconsider how close you want to keep that friend. You might not want to end the friendship entirely, but you can limit the amount of time you spend with them.

Trying to figure out how to make a friendship work or deciding whether to end it may require a lot of deliberation, especially if you've been friends for years. Some disagreements between friends are inevitable, but ultimately friendship is meant to be nourishing rather than destructive. Jealousy is a common struggle, but I hope you and your friends don't allow disappointments to sabotage what could be a really good friendship. We can all grow in our level of self-awareness, build a life that feels fulfilling, and celebrate and love our friends well.

SIGNS THAT A STRONG FRIEND IS STRUGGLING

Another common dynamic is when one of the friends is the "strong one" in a relationship—someone known for being highly capable and resilient. It can be tempting to put someone in a box and assume that they're always strong, but the truth is, we're all human, so be mindful of when your friends might be overwhelmed, so you can show up for them.

What are some signs that your strong friend might be struggling? People who are used to being strong often try to manage their distress by diving even deeper into their work and by becoming even more of a workaholic or perfectionist. If your friend seems busier than usual, recognize their humanity and understand that many people may rely on them. Tune in to what it must feel like for them to receive constant requests for support. Instead of thinking about their efficiency and capacity to be of service to you, separate yourself from the crowd of people heaping respon-sibilities on them and show up for them instead.

You might have a hard time recalling the last time you heard this friend acknowledge their own humanity, fatigue, or limita-tions. In the context of your friendship, think about whether they ever share vulnerably. If not, ask yourself: *Do I communicate in ways that make them feel pressured to perform rather than connecting authentically as friends?* People often operate based on what they think others expect of them, so if your friend always acts as though everything is fine or under control, or if they never share anything that isn't superficial, then you may want to check in with them and think about how you can communicate with them in a way that would shift the tide. If you notice that your strong friend is going into overdrive and never shares vulnerably in your presence, these may be signs that you could do a better job of checking in with them.

If you notice that your strong friend is disappearing all the time, showing up only when they aren't struggling, because they don't want to be a burden or because they believe that others won't show up for them, this may be a sign that they are over-whelmed or in crisis. If your friend who is usually supportive, vo-cal, and in the middle of the action suddenly goes quiet, don't keep pulling on them to be the cheerleader or the entertainer of the group. Instead, rally your friend group around this person so you all can be a resource and support for them.

When a strong friend is feeling overwhelmed, they may be-come increasingly irritable, short-tempered, or impatient. They may become resentful about taking care of everything for every-one else when they themselves are struggling and no one notices or shows up for them. Others may even assume they just have a bad attitude or are really negative. Resist the urge to jump to conclusions and see if there's a story or pattern behind the change in behavior—it could be a sign of distress.

Be especially mindful of your friend if they are going through a life transition or challenge like losing a loved one. Even if they haven't complained or verbally expressed any difficulty, think about what's on their plate and how most people might find it challenging, and respond accordingly. Even if they're going through a change that isn't necessarily negative, like a job transition, a new relationship, a move, or a promotion, they might be under more stress than usual, so be attentive to what your friend might be carrying in this season.

Pay particular attention if your friend doesn't look like themselves. If your friend feels on top of things, they might show up in public in a way that reflects that, but if they feel overwhelmed (even if they don't say so aloud), you might be able to tell by their facial expression or the way they aren't taking care of their skin or hair or dressing the way they normally would. Often those who are used to being the strong one in a relationship will neglect themselves while taking care of everyone else.

Be mindful if you are in a friend group where many people are struggling and depending on one person in particular. The strong friend might be carrying too much—not just for their friends but for their parents, children, and job. If you notice that no one is caring for them or pouring into them, don't ignore this sign but be a part of shifting the dynamic.

Another sign that your strong friend might be in need of support is if they disappear from social media, or if their social media posts directly communicate or have an undercurrent suggesting that all is not well. Don't ignore these messages, even if your friend never expresses these problems to you in person, and don't just wait for their behavior to change on its own. Offer support to your friend even if it turns out they don't need it, because friendship should always be a mutually caring relationship.

Catilina is a Latina woman in her late forties who recently went through a divorce due to her husband's infidelity and emotional abuse. She is devastated by the response of her friends. She feels she has cultivated and invested more in their mutual friends and assumed they would be on her side. Her ex-husband has quickly entered a new relationship, proposed, and set the date for his wedding. She is appalled that their mutual friends have agreed to attend the wedding. She is struggling to honor her feelings, needs, and expectations regarding friendship.

HOW TO HELP A FRIEND IN NEED

What are some ways that you can check in and be supportive of a strong friend? You can start by directly asking, "How have things been for you?" Avoid the brief scripted exchange of "How are you?" followed by an automatic "Fine, how are you?" by really slowing down and sharing your observations: "I know you have a lot on your plate, so what has that been like for you? What's been helpful and what's been challenging about this season?" By asking more specific questions with compassion and without judgment, you're more likely to get an honest answer. You can also ask how you can support them. If they're overwhelmed or aren't used to asking for help, you can offer something specific based on what you've observed and know of them. What could you offer that would bring them joy or make them feel more relaxed? Which of their responsibilities could you help with? You could offer both emotional and practical support by being a safe place where they can vent as well as helping them with family obligations, financial responsibilities, or creative endeavors. Your actions should be aligned with your words of support.

You can also encourage your friend to set boundaries, including with you. If you have a lot on your mind, ask if they have the time and capacity to hear about it before you unload on them. If it is not the right time and place, you can save your news for later. Encouraging your friend to exercise stronger boundaries with you and others requires you to have healthy boundaries yourself. If you notice that your friend never says no to anyone, you could plant this seed: "Sometimes we need to say no so we can say yes to ourselves, our rest, and the things we have already agreed to do. I wonder if there are any things you feel like saying no to in this season." You could also ask your friend what might make it hard for them to say no to some people and then brainstorm with them about how to work through those challenges together.

By respecting your friend's boundaries, you're showing them that you are looking out for them. If you often rely on the same person for support, work to identify other resources. This doesn't mean that you can never confide in your friend again, but you might think about getting mental health support from a professional. You don't want to go to your friend only in times of crisis; otherwise, they may think, *If _____ is reaching out, it must mean that they need something from me.* It's helpful to have different people that you can reach out to when you need support, and make sure you're sharing joy and laughter, not just your problems, with your friends.

Finally, encourage your friend to exercise self-care. Since people who are used to being the strong one in a relationship often neglect themselves, help your strong friend to set boundaries and urge them to do things that bring them joy, peace, and a sense of personal fulfillment. They shouldn't do things solely because they're trying to help other people. Our strong friends may need to hear that they aren't simply an instrument to help others; they, too, are deserving of kindness, respect, love, compassion, rest, and abundance.

LEARNING FROM PAST RELATIONSHIPS

Every relationship is bound to experience tension at some point, so rather than panicking or freezing in the face of conflict, try to be present for it and process it with the goal of developing a stronger friendship. The same tools we use to resolve disagreements with friends apply to relationships of all kinds, including family, romantic partners, colleagues, neighbors, and members of our faith community. I want to be clear that it is necessary to leave abusive relationships, but this chapter focuses on friendships where we can address conflict in healthy ways, heal, and strengthen the relationship.

In this moment, I invite you to reflect on your own journey and how you've resolved conflict in the past. What life experiences affected the way you handle conflict? Growing up, how did you see your family resolve conflict? What messages did you receive in school about resolving conflict? Think about your history of friendship. What has it looked like when friendships ended? Why and how did they end? When we are unable to resolve conflicts with friends, this can cause a great deal of distress and anxiety, lead us to act in unhealthy ways toward others and ourselves, and sabotage relationships we value. What do you tend to do when you experience disappointments or disagreements? What can you observe about how other people respond to you in the midst of conflict? As you've experienced growth in your healing journey, have you noticed changes in the way you handle conflict?

We want to be tuned in to our own issues, baggage, and patterns of behavior. When we are honest with ourselves, we can start to recognize areas where we feel good about how we've addressed conflict in the past, as well as moments when we know we did not handle the situation well or honor ourselves, the other person, or the process. We acknowledge our weaknesses, not to beat ourselves up but to pinpoint areas of growth so we can work on them.

Still Waters is a Native American man who had a rupture with his best friend. The best friend shared early on that she had a romantic interest in him, but the feeling was not mutual. He expressed his desire for them to remain friends. She interpreted/ misinterpreted his kindness and investment of time as movement toward a relationship. When he shared that he had begun dating someone, his dear friend was heartbroken and cut off communication. They were both hurting, angry, disappointed, and confused. They needed to talk both to clear the air regarding the past and to determine what, if anything, was possible for their friendship in the present. In the end, his friend decided it was too painful for her to remain friends with him, but they resolved the hurt feelings by acknowledging they had both been honest and showed care for each other.

STEPS TO RESOLVE CONFLICT

The first step in resolving conflict is to really understand yourself and your emotions. When you find yourself getting upset because someone has said or done something that you find offensive or disrespectful or otherwise don't like, reflect on exactly what bothers you and how it makes you feel. Give yourself permission to acknowledge a range of feelings. Some of us may have a one-note response, going from neutral to angry when triggered. If the only emotion you can tap into is anger, you may want to reflect on why that is and uncover any other emotions beneath the anger.

Other people have a tendency to feel hurt when they encounter conflict. If they have a difference of opinion with someone else, they may see this as a personal slight or attack. If we interpret every disagreement to mean that the other person doesn't like us, this can leave us feeling hurt most of the time, and our relationships become fragile.

Still other people may shut down in the face of tension. They may feel numb when they're slighted. When others ask if they're upset, they'll respond with something like "I don't care" as a form of armor, leaving no room to communicate or heal the rupture because they've convinced themselves that they don't care, when deep down they really do. Similarly, people may respond to conflict with avoidance. They are quick to be done with the situation, so there's no space for dialogue.

We must examine our responses to conflict and get a sense of what we are really feeling and why. Let's ask ourselves: Does this moment represent something more to me than what is really happening in the present? Conflict can create a wave of emotions, so it's central for us to understand its intensity and the reasons for it. When we are self-aware and communicate our experiences with the other person, they, too, can better understand the intensity of what we're feeling.

For example, if you have a history of people not listening to you or talking over you—perhaps you had a partner who did that and was toxic and emotionally abusive—you may feel triggered if a new friend gets excited and begins talking over you. While it's crucial to give people space to communicate without interrupting them, if your immediate reaction is at a level 10, it might be less about what this particular person has done than the cumulative effect of all the other times someone has spoken over you and you froze or didn't defend yourself. You may be in warrior mode now because you never want to experience that again.

When we find ourselves feeling triggered, we must ask: Is this about the present or the past? Is the present moment reminding me of the past? Why does this interaction feel so charged? Where is the intensity coming from? Self-understanding is essential to engaging in conflict resolution.

It is also key to learn how to regulate our emotions and self-soothe when we're upset. When we're facing a difficult situation on our own, we need to be able to comfort ourselves and give ourselves permission to breathe and feel whatever we're feeling. If you're in the middle of a conflict with a friend, you can't depend on the other person to calm or soothe you, because they're also upset. As with any caring relationship, we want to be able to love and comfort each other, but in the heat of the moment when we're at odds with each other, we each need to be able to self-regulate and find clarity within ourselves. You are responsible for checking in with yourself and calming yourself, and hopefully your friend is doing the same. While tension is inevitable in any relationship, it doesn't have to become explosive; we don't have to default to warrior mode.

The time we need to reflect and self-soothe varies from person to person. Some people immediately recognize when they've said something that was uncalled for. They may follow it right away with "Oh, I shouldn't have said that. It wasn't really about you. I'm upset about something that happened earlier, and you reminded me of that person." Other people may need more of a sacred pause, in which case they might respond with something like "I want to talk, but I need to take a walk to clear my head first. If it works for you, can we continue this conversation when I get back?" Honor your process and your friend's process. Some of us prefer to talk it out immediately, staying up until all hours of the night to resolve the situation. Other people prefer to sleep on it, journal, take a walk, and reflect. No two people are identical, so we need to learn to compromise.

I also invite you to frame these discussions as concerns rather than attacks or critiques of your friend. Explain how their words or actions made you feel rather than making assumptions about their intentions, overgeneralizing, or resorting to name-calling. When you raise a concern, be specific about something that has been said or done. If you're addressing a pattern of behavior, name examples of when it's come up, but don't overgeneralize by saying, "This is who you are." Such a statement is a form of name-calling and can cause the other person to become defensive instead of hearing your concern. A true invitation to dialogue allows both people to reflect and talk about how they can improve the relationship and communicate better, so respectfully share your concern rather than attack.

Resolving conflict requires prioritizing the friendship rather trying to prove that you're right. If I'm just trying to win an argument, I don't have to show any concern for the other person or their feelings, perspective, or experience. But if I value the friendship enough to keep working on it and I want *us* to win rather than *me* to win, then I'll be more careful with my language. My tone should communicate care and respect, inviting my friend to honestly share their opinion even if it differs from my perspective. Inviting a friend to share their views doesn't mean that I have to stay silent or censor myself, but my words and actions should be guided by the fact that I'm not here to fight but to create a way forward.

Each person should feel safe to speak their truth in a friendship, so I need to create an environment where I am approachable. Even if I don't explicitly silence people with my words, I should discern whether any of my behaviors suggest to my friend that I don't want to hear their opinion—indeed, that there is no room for feelings, thoughts, or needs other than my own. I have to ask myself: How do I respond when a friend says that I have offended, hurt, or disrespected them in some way? Am I able to hear other people's concerns? Am I someone who can never apologize? Do I tend to go into attack mode? If a friend raises a current concern, do I respond by bringing up ten things they've done in the past that I didn't like? When I think about my friendships in general, am I approachable? Am I accessible? Do other people feel like they can talk to me? If not, this will create a disconnect with my friends.

One of the ways in which we can shut other people down is with our rage. If you respond to a friend's concern by going into a rage, this is a form of manipulation that is meant to silence them. It communicates that they can never disagree with you.

We can also shut people down by giving them the silent treatment. This is different from letting them know that you need to take a sacred pause before resuming the conversation; the silent treatment shuts down all communication. If a friend raises an issue with you, how do you let them know that you have the emotional capacity and willingness to hear what they have to say and that you can own your part in a conflict? Healing ruptures in friendships requires both people to reflect on how they've contributed to the tension through their words and actions, including their silence. If you've never voiced or communicated a preference or expectation, you can't blame your friends for not knowing it, even if you wish they had guessed it.

If your friend deserves an apology, share a sincere and specific apology, not just something perfunctory like "Sorry if you were hurt" or "Sorry if I bothered you." The apology should communicate your awareness of how your words or actions impacted your friend as well as your commitment to not saying or doing those things again.

Lastly, conflict resolution requires follow-up. In the immediate aftermath, people may feel like they've talked it through, but then as more time passes, it's valuable to check in again rather than hoping or assuming that the conflict is completely behind you. You might say, "I know we had that difficult conversation, and I feel like we came to a solution, but I just wanted to check and see how you've been feeling since then."

Conflict resolution can be challenging, but it's essential for our growth personally and in relationship with those we care about. Each person has their own history and challenges, so there's no expectation of perfection in how we interact with others, but we can honor our friends by showing up and letting them know: "I value this relationship, and I want to make it better. I want to be a part of the solution."

Conflict resolution requires humility and a real effort to listen, own our issues, and share vulnerably, but deep, committed friendships that stand the test of time are 100 percent worth it.

Angela had a lot of one-sided friendships and connections with relatives. She came to therapy with a lot of resentment, fatigue, and disappointment. She couldn't understand why she gave everything to her friends but they rarely reciprocated. In therapy she came to see her pattern of taking on everyone else's challenges but hiding her own. She thought about which friends she believed really didn't have the capacity to support her and acknowledged that a few of them possibly could but she had never given them the chance. She began to open up more, ask for help, and set boundaries about not always trying to rescue them. While a few disappointed her, a couple of them emerged as sincerely available and their friendships grew. She is relieved that she released some unhealthy connections and opened her heart to deeper mutual friendship with others.

ACTIVATION EXERCISE: Have a conversation with a friend or write them a letter reflecting on a prior rupture that occurred in the friendship. If there is anything that has been unspoken that you would like to share, feel free to share it. If you appreciate the ways you both addressed the issue at the time, communicate that gratitude. Reflection and awareness help friendships to grow and hearts to heal.

AFFIRMATION: If it aligns with you, hold one hand with the other and speak the words "I have the maturity to talk through difficult issues and work toward resolution."

14

HEALING WITHOUT AN APOLOGY

Ha is an Asian American woman in her late thirties. Her mother was physically, verbally, and emotionally abusive. Ha suspects her mother is narcissistic but doesn't know for sure, since her mother has always refused to go to therapy. Her mother remains emotionally and verbally abusive and never apologizes. While Ha has created boundaries regarding visits with her mother, she still desires some form of a relationship with her. She would like to heal her heart so the wounds from her mother's abuse don't continue to hinder her self-love or her ability to have a loving relationship.

f a family member, friend, or partner broke your trust, you may feel stuck dealing with the consequences of their actions, especially if they refused to take responsibility. You may have spent a lot of time waiting and hoping that they would apologize and change. I want you to know that regardless of whether you ever receive the apology you deserve, you can live a full life with a healed heart. It's time to take your life off hold and take ownership of your own healing.

REFLECTING ON HOW YOU'VE BEEN WRONGED

I invite you to pause and reflect for a moment on a time when you were wronged and didn't receive an apology. Some of you may be experiencing that right now, so that instance came to mind as soon as you saw the title of this chapter. For others, the offense, the violation, or the hurt happened a long time ago, and now you're wrestling with what to do with the added injury of never having received an apology. This reflection exercise may require some of you to get in touch with the impact of your experience, to come to a place of truth-telling, perhaps admitting for the first time that it hurt. Previously you may have said, "I don't care," or "It doesn't matter," or "I don't even think about that." You might constantly think about the person who wronged you without giving any thought to yourself, your heart, and the impact of their words or behavior on your well-being.

We need to tune in to how wounds show up in our lives, because it can look different for each person and scenario. A wound may show up as depression or anxiety or shame. If we're not tuned in to our emotions, a wound may manifest itself as sabotaging, isolating, withdrawing, or behaving aggressively. A wound may show up in people-pleasing, perfectionism, or busyness. It may show up in nightmares or insomnia. Or it may show up in a compromised immune system, because the body perpetually feels the weight of the wound even if we haven't fully acknowledged it to ourselves. Acknowledging the wound is a central part of the healing process.

WHY DON'T PEOPLE APOLOGIZE?

There are several reasons why someone might not apologize. An authentic apology requires self-awareness and emotional maturity, and many people have not developed the emotional capacity to confess their wrongdoing. It takes emotional strength and humility to look at the ways in which we've fallen short or done things that we regret that have hurt other people. For some, it might be much easier to sit with the ways in which others have wronged them than to acknowledge the wrongs they themselves have committed. Other people can acknowledge wrongdoing privately within themselves, but have a harder time taking the additional step of confessing it aloud.

Still others don't apologize simply because they aren't sorry. They may feel justified in their actions because you also did something wrong; they may feel that what they did was a lesser or equal wrong compared to what you did, so they don't think they owe you an apology. Some people don't think they've done anything wrong because they're unable or unwilling to engage in perspective-taking—that is, looking at something from someone else's point of view. If someone's response to hurting you is "I didn't do it on purpose" or "You're being sensitive. I was just being honest," then they are unable to pivot from their own perspective to how you felt and experienced their words or actions. It might be helpful for them to consider: Is there another way that I could have said or gone about that? Were my words or actions even necessary? Answering those questions requires perspective-taking and compassion.

Some people won't apologize because they were raised or taught through prior relationships to believe that apologies aren't necessary. They may never have had anyone model sincere apologies, so they just move on and act as though nothing happened. Some couples "apologize" to each other without explicitly saying sorry. Instead, they'll say things like "Do you want to go get something to eat?" "Do you want to come watch TV with me?" or "Do you want to cuddle?" Their definition of an apology is simply changing the subject and moving on. The person who was wronged might still be waiting for a real apology, while the other person assumes that the issue is behind them. If the person who was wronged brings it up in conversation, the other person might respond with "Oh, you're still mad about that?" even though they never apologized.

Other people might not apologize because they think it to be a sign of weakness. Perhaps past experience has taught them that if they apologize, it gives other people fuel to use against them. They may have experienced people repeatedly bringing up a past wrong, so they want to avoid having their mistakes thrown back in their faces. They think that any admission of wrongdoing could be used as ammunition against them, so they choose to deny, deny, deny. Even if they are caught in a lie, they continue to lie. Even if they've been caught doing something that is out of order, they refuse to acknowledge wrongdoing and hope to escape without consequences.

TAKING YOUR HEALING INTO YOUR OWN HANDS

Whatever the reason may be for why someone hasn't apologized to you, I want you to know that you have been wronged, hurt, abused, misused, discarded, or abandoned, and that you deserve better. No one deserves mistreatment or abuse or violation of any kind. We do not deserve disrespect.

I also want you to weigh the impact of waiting for the apology in order to heal. What might happen if you don't take your healing into your own hands and, instead, leave your healing in the hands of those who harmed you, waiting for them to stitch you back together again? Who is continuing to be harmed by your disengagement with your healing process? If you wait for people to explain to you why they hurt you, then you are putting your healing journey on pause. You cannot move forward until someone else offers an explanation and an apology. This is like remaining in a box and giving the person who hurt you the key, saying, "Only when they decide I can get out of this box will I begin to live again."

Many of us have wasted months, years, and lifetimes waiting for those who harmed us to bring us medicine, waiting for those who carry a dagger in their hand to give us roses. I want you to know that you are deserving of healing. Although the harm was out of your hands, your wholeness is very much in them. Your journey, your process, and your recovery are truly yours for the taking.

Frame it as a radical act of love to love yourself more than those who hurt you. The person who wronged you may not have cared about you, or perhaps they did care about you, but just not as much as they cared about themselves, their ego, their needs, their priorities, and their desires.

Today, we have the power to decide: I love myself enough to take control of my life. I love myself enough to invest in my healing. I love myself enough to claim my power. I refuse to live the rest of my life waiting. I take back my life—my body, my mind, my heart, my spirit, my time. I'm picking up the discarded pieces and choosing myself. I'm no longer waiting for the parent who abandoned me to choose me, for the partner who rejected me to choose me, for the stranger on the street who violated, disrespected, and dishonored me to choose me. I'm no longer waiting for my supervisor, coworker, relative, ex-friend, frenemy, or enemy to decide that I deserve their apology. I am choosing and loving myself because I see how necessary it is. I am no longer willing to pay the price of self-neglect, self-abandonment, powerlessness, and waiting. We respond to ourselves with tenderness and compassion, as well as a sense of urgency, because the waiting is disempowering;

it only magnifies the wound to wait for someone to give you what you can give yourself.

I want to note that there is a difference between accepting an apology and reconciling with someone. Some of you might find it difficult to heal because you are continuing to center the person who is hurting you. It is much easier to heal a wound without an apology if you disengage or find some emotional and physical distance from the person who has wronged you. But if you continue to give that person full access to your time, energy, and emotions, then it will be hard to heal because they are continuing to harm you.

Be mindful of how much access you give to someone who continues to hurt you. There's a difference between healing a past wound and healing an ongoing one. Ask yourself: Is this wound ongoing? If so, you need to think not only about your healing but also about your self-preservation and self-protection. What can you do to reduce your interaction with people who continue to hurt you without apology?

Those of us who are healing a past wound—whether from childhood or last year or last month—must shift to the present and stop replaying past events over and over again in our heads. When we get to a place of radical acceptance, we think: *I didn't like what happened, and I didn't want it to happen, but it happened. And no matter how many times I replay it in my mind, no matter how much regret or shame I feel, I cannot change the past.*

I invite you to give yourself permission to show up for your present. While our healing does involve looking back, that does not mean living back. Some of us are living in the past, reliving it every day. If that's the case for you, gradually move toward placing more of your focus on the present. Presence is a gift that you can give yourself. Do some perspective-taking to understand who you were at that time, and if you have insight into it, who the person who wronged you was at the time. Some of us stay locked in past wounds because we believe that on some level we were deserving of the mistreatment or we feel that we are unworthy of love, care, and respect. If I believe that the wrong done against me says something about me, it will be hard to heal because I am holding on to a distorted idea of myself. I have given meaning to violations against me and allowed those experiences to define me. So I invite you to consider that just because something happened to you, this does not mean that you deserved it, and it does not define who you are. When we take in this reality, we can begin to shift, break through, unleash and unlock ourselves from the lies that the mistreatment told us about who we are and what we deserve.

Louis is an African American man in his mid-twenties. He is heartbroken. In college, he met the woman of his dreams. He found her to be incredibly attractive, kind, and fun. They started dating their last year of college. After graduation, they ended up in different cities. She went to graduate school and he accepted a job offer. Louis was planning to propose and imagined their lives together. The second time he went to visit her, he had planned lots of romantic outings. Unfortunately, the first night together, she announced that they were too young to be this serious and that the long-distance relationship wasn't working for her. She wanted them to be nonexclusive and date other people. When Louis expressed his hurt feelings and desire to remain committed, his girlfriend said he was being "selfish, immature, and ridiculous." It's been two years since they have spoken, and Louis feels stuck and incapable of trust or love.

I invite you to step out of your fantasy world and begin creating the life you want. If I am waiting for an apology, I can get stuck in the hope and dream of what could have been if people had treated me differently. I can get stuck wishing that my parents had really been loving toward me, or that my former partner had wanted to stay with me. What if, what if, what if? What if the supervisor who overlooked me would come to their senses and realize that I'm the best person for the promotion? We can get stuck in fantasies, wishing to be seen and treated differently.

Grieve the fantasy of what could have been; grieve the dreams that didn't come to fruition. Grieving is an essential part of the healing process and ultimately gets us to the place of accepting the reality and shifting into creating the life we want rather than waiting for other people to hand us the life we desired.

As you are seeking to free yourself from the past, it can also be helpful to write the apology you wish you had received. When you write down what you hoped they would say, it can give you insight into the places where you may be stuck.

If I am waiting for them to say that I didn't deserve it, is a part of me wondering if I deserved it?

If I am waiting for them to say that they really did care about me, are there parts of me who feel like I abandoned myself? Are there ways in which I need to nurture, nourish, love, and care for myself more boldly and courageously?

What are the words you are longing to hear from others? To the extent that you can, give yourself whatever you're longing to receive from others. We can love, choose, and prioritize ourselves in the ways we wish other people had. In so doing, we can move toward our healing, our wellness, and our restoration.

Your physical, mental, emotional, and spiritual health can all be harmed by waiting for an apology that is not coming. For the sake of your healing and restoration, make a decision to choose you. I know this is easier said than done, that it's not as simple as just reading this chapter, but we are all on this healing journey together, so let's not wait for the people who hurt us to give us the ticket to our healing.

Isabella is in her early thirties. She has some friends and has had some romantic partners. These connections never last. Isabella felt stuck in feelings of unworthiness stemming from her mother's physically and psychologically abusive behaviors and her father's abandonment. She has been waiting for her parents to acknowledge and apologize for the hurt they caused. She has also been waiting for her other relatives who knew about the abuse and abandonment to acknowledge it. In therapy, she had to grieve and release the fantasy of her mother's and father's transformation and her extended family's admissions. Isabella began focusing on nourishing and loving herself and choosing friends and dating partners who align with her care and flourishing. She had to end the tendency to break off female friendships too fast and to hold on to harmful romantic partners too long. She now has two positive female friends and is finally taking a break from dating to heal and restore herself. She feels that with more clarity and healing, she will be able to exhibit healthier decision-making and discernment.

ACTIVATION EXERCISE: Create a "healing your heart" playlist. Include songs about healing, hope, and love. Play the music when you feel moved to hear it, but at least once a week. Let the message minister to your heart.

AFFIRMATION: If it aligns with you, place both hands on your heart and complete the following phrases aloud:

I release _____

I make room for _____

I release _____

I receive _____

I release _____

I am free to _____

And so it is.

15

RELEASING SOMEONE WHO DOESN'T LOVE YOU

Brenda is a divorced African American woman in her forties. She was approached and pursued by an African American man who is also in his forties. Initially she was hesitant due to past hurts in relationships, including an unhealthy marriage. Eventually she let her guard down and expressed that the feelings of attraction and connection were mutual. The gentleman then announced that he was not ready for a relationship and proceeded to send various mixed signals. None of these signals led to any progress toward a committed relationship. Brenda was confused and heartbroken. She tried to figure out how to fix things, as she felt the connection was genuine. Eventually she had to allow herself to grieve and release, acknowledging that the person who approached her never had genuine intentions.

It's incredibly painful to love someone who doesn't reciprocate your feelings—at least not to the same extent. Perhaps the most challenging part of all is accepting the truth that your love is unrequited. How do you release someone who does not love you back?

Before we address this question, I invite you to tune in to your breath. The very idea of being unloved by someone for whom you care deeply can create a lot of physical, emotional, and spiritual tension in your body. You may have been holding yourself rigidly in denial or hope, or trying to block out the disappointment. Although the truth can be painful, it is ultimately best to live a life rooted in the truth.

ACCEPTING THE TRUTH

If the truth is that someone does not love you the way you want and deserve to be loved, then it's time to think about letting go. This may involve a grieving process—grieving over disappointed hopes, dreams, and desires—and getting to a place of radical truth-telling. As we accept the reality, we recognize that this process is not really about releasing the person, because they were never truly with us on an emotional level if they didn't love us. While it might be painful to think about how they were never really present with us in the ways that we needed, truth-telling is our path to liberation.

Give yourself permission and space to acknowledge the person or people who didn't reciprocate your love. By accepting what you have experienced, you are embracing reality rather than scrounging for scraps of evidence that they are deserving of your love. People call it bread-crumbing when someone gives you just enough to keep you holding on, but if you step back and look at the big picture—including what the person has told you and how they've treated you—the truth is this is not love, and you know it. So we breathe and accept the truth that our love is not reciprocated. The pathway to our healing is in our commitment not to deceive ourselves, not to live a life based on delusion or illusion, but to be courageous enough to see things as they are.

Another valuable aspect of telling ourselves the truth is to be honest about how we feel about the other person. If they don't love us, we might try to convince ourselves that we don't love them, either, but this might not be the case. In this moment, even as you acknowledge that someone doesn't love you, can you give yourself the gift of honesty and say that you are aware of your own feelings for them? We cannot cope with reality, process our emotions, or heal when we are deceiving ourselves. Regardless of what you have said to your friends, family, or directly to this person, tell yourself the truth about how you feel in this moment.

ONE-SIDED RELATIONSHIPS ARE NOT ENOUGH

Malcolm is a married mixed-race man who is in a loveless marriage. He gives to his wife emotionally and financially, but she never reciprocates. His family and friends have tried to speak with him about it, but he gets angry whenever the topic of his marriage comes up. His wife picked him because he represented financial security and because she was getting older and was worried about her biological clock running out before she had children. Now she has the finances and children but feels it is not enough. She regrets saying yes to the marriage. Malcolm has tried for years to win the heart of his wife with no progress. He has decided it's time to heal his heart and has requested to go to couples counseling or separate.

With emotional intelligence, we recognize that our feelings alone are not a sufficient foundation for a relationship. This is true of relationships of all kinds—with friends, family members, and romantic partners. A one-sided relationship is not going to work, so regardless of my feelings for another person—whether romantic or platonic, or with a family member—I don't get to dictate how they feel about me. Whatever my hopes may be for this mother-daughter relationship or this dynamic with my siblings or this level of intimacy with my partner, the truth is that how these people have responded to me, spoken to me, and spoken about me lets me know that they may not see the relationship in the same way I do. I must acknowledge the truth of their feelings or lack thereof. I also acknowledge the truth about what I've felt or feel, and then I accept the fact that my feelings alone are insufficient for the flourishing of the friendship, romantic relationship, or familial connection—I cannot carry the relationship by myself.

People sometimes think that if they just love someone enough, they can convince that person to love them back. I want you to know that love does not require convincing. Of course those who have harmed a relationship by breaking the other person's trust must be held accountable for their actions, but with the exception of this kind of scenario, we shouldn't have to convince other people that we're worthy of their love and care. Love shows up with open hands, open hearts, and open eyes to see you.

We release the false belief that it is our job to convince others that we deserve their love and care. Some of us may have received that script as children—we may have been raised in a way that taught us that we had to prove our worth. If you have an anxious or insecure attachment style, you may need to remind yourself that you are already enough. The right people will align themselves with you, choose you, and love you without requiring you to contort or erase yourself.

PRACTICAL NEXT STEPS

Lisa is a thirty-five-year-old Latina who has been living with Jeremy for seven years. She wants to get married, and he has put it off, noting that he wants to make more money before marriage and saying he is not sure she has all the attributes he is looking for. Lisa feels like their relationship has been one long audition, with her never getting the part. He recently told her he is moving out and moving on. Lisa is devastated. She feels she gave him the best years of her life and cannot imagine what life can look like at this point.

It is time to cut off access with unloving people. If someone fundamentally does not care about you, respect you, or love you, you will need to create some space between you and that person. Sometimes people try to convince themselves that receiving unkind behavior is okay, that they don't mind, and that they can adjust, but the reality is that their hearts are continuing to break. We may need to wean ourselves from the attention of the person who has hurt us. We may need to set an intention to not occupy our thoughts and time with monitoring that person on social media or desperately reaching out. Rather, we must prioritize our own healing and wellness. It is very hard to heal in the presence of someone who does not care, respect, or love us, because making space for them requires us to diminish ourselves. If we feel dishonored by someone's presence or interactions with us, then we give ourselves permission to reclaim our energy, focus, and time so we can protect our peace.

It can be helpful in terms of accountability to share where you are in this process with someone you trust. Sometimes we know what we need to do but we are not always disciplined in following through. We may not be rooted firmly enough in awareness and self-love to be able to hold our boundaries with other people. In instances like these, it helps to have a friend, family member, or therapist in whom you can confide what you're feeling and what you've observed; then this person can help you follow through on your intention to honor yourself. We share our convictions with them in our moments of strength so they can help us walk that out in our moments of struggle. We reach out to them so they can reflect our truths back to us when we need to hear them. They remind us that we are worthy of love, care, and respect.

Be intentional about showering yourself with care and love. In moments of struggle, you might think you just need to distract yourself with someone else. If someone doesn't want to be my friend, I might turn immediately to the next person I meet to be my best friend, directing all my time and energy at them. If this parenting or sibling relationship hasn't turned out the way I hoped, I might be tempted to start love-bombing someone after a first date. I might start looking to them to take the place of the family member who didn't show up for me. Rather than shifting all our needs and energy into a new person, we want to take time to nourish, care for, and love ourselves. Can you take the love that you were so ready and willing to pour into another person and instead pour it into yourself? Can you start to attend to your own voice and needs? Can you start to cultivate joy in your life?

While we need to grieve our disappointments, we also want to think about how to bring joy into our lives in ways not dependent on another person's loving us. What are my pathways to joy outside of this person?

What are some ways you can give yourself rest? What are some ways you can give yourself joy? What are some ways you can give yourself delight? What are some ways you can give yourself fun? Can you take yourself out on a date night? What would you like to do this week? What would you enjoy? As you become more firmly rooted in who you are, independent of anyone else, I hope you learn to create joyful moments and experiences for yourself and with yourself.

Being at home in ourselves is not just about releasing but also receiving, and receiving doesn't require us to wait for someone else to bring us joy. What are the ways in which you feel empowered to bring joy into your week? How can you be mindful and intentional about expressing love for yourself?

Finally, I invite you to reflect. What did you gain from the experience of releasing this person? What do you now know that you didn't know before? Wisdom is a gift. While we hope that we won't encounter the same situation again in the future, we want to have a solid understanding of what we learned about what love feels like and, conversely, what a lack of love feels like.

Jeremiah had to reconcile himself to the fact that his father doesn't care about him. Jeremiah had tried to win his father's approval with success in sports, and when that didn't work and he didn't make it to the pros, he tried to win his father over with gifts and money. He always ended up feeling used and taken for granted, and less and less time would pass before his father made a new financial demand. Jeremiah realized how much time and energy he has spent trying to win the love of his father, all to no avail. His father has never been invested in him. Jeremiah thought he had to hold on to his father because so many people wish they knew their father. He finally admitted to himself that his father's discarding of him has been his biggest heartbreak. He realizes he has participated in the pattern by allowing it to continue. Now in his late thirties, Jeremiah has felt ready to stop running every time his father calls with a new demand. He is disappointed to note that as he has stopped helping his father financially, his father is reaching out to him less frequently. Ultimately, though, Jeremiah feels that seeing the truth has set him free.

ACTIVATION EXERCISE: Journal about the following questions. As you've reflected, what did you discover was at the root of your trying to convince people who don't love you to love you? How does this require your attention and healing? What did you learn about your friends based on those you felt you could share your disappointments with? Were there those you could not trust these tender parts of your heart with? What does this say about your friendships? What did you discover about your own capacity to release people and to accept truth even when it's painful? Have you made some progress there? Do you see growth in yourself? What are some ways in which you could continue to grow? What makes you more vulnerable to lying to yourself? What empowers you to recognize and accept the truth even when it is not what you want to hear?

AFFIRMATION: These can be challenging questions to ponder. Take a cleansing breath and say aloud, "I am lovable and worthy of care and respect."

16

HEALING CONTROL ISSUES

Salim is a married Palestinian man and father of four. He has faced a lot of loss in his life. His parents and siblings were all killed. He feels guilt for living away from his country and wonders if he had been there if he could have saved some of them. He lives with a lot of fear of his family being unsafe. He manages his anxiety by being very strict with his children and by discouraging his wife from activities outside of the home. His control issues also show up at work. He is afraid of being anything less than perfect because he doesn't want to feed into the stereotypes that many having regarding Arab Americans and Middle Easterners. He hasn't found coworkers or supervisors to be trustworthy enough and feels he has to do everything on his own. His supervisor has said he needs to work on being a team player. His wife sees how he is struggling and filled with fear and grief. At her suggestion, he has agreed to couples counseling.

Often, when the topic of control issues comes up, we're describing someone else's problem. We may not see or acknowledge our own issues with needing to be in control of everything and everyone. Or perhaps you recognize your desire for control, or maybe other people have told you that you can be controlling. If any of this resonates with you, I invite you to dive deeper into this chapter as we explore how to heal and release that need for control so that we can live freer lives and be more at peace within ourselves and with other people.

THE ROOTS OF CONTROL ISSUES

There are many different reasons why people struggle with control issues. If you experienced physical or emotional neglect as a child, you likely had to grow up quickly and figure out how to take care of yourself and others. The term *parentified child* refers to a child who feels responsible for taking care of their parents. If you are an older sibling, you may have felt responsible for taking care of your younger siblings. Even middle or younger children sometimes take on the role of peacemaker in their families. Perhaps you had to provide for your family financially or materially when you were very young. These kinds of experiences may ingrain in you the idea that you cannot trust other people to handle these responsibilities. You may internalize the belief that you have to do everything yourself because if you are not on top of it all, everything will fall apart.

Others develop a need for control after experiencing trauma. Whether you experienced a medical trauma, child abuse, sexual abuse or assault, or the murder of a loved one, or witnessed family violence, these events were out of your control. As a result, you may associate not being in control with bad things happening, so you try to be in control at all times in order to stay safe.

Sometimes it's not just the traumatic event that makes you feel out of control, but also the responses of other people. If you see people blame the victim for their experience, then you may internalize the idea that you are responsible for other people's behavior. Whether you received that message directly or indirectly, you may develop a sense of responsibility for everything and everyone. When things don't go well, regardless of the specifics of the situation, you may believe that it is your fault. As a result, you may try to be perfect and make everything go as perfectly as possible.

The experience of being dominated or controlled by another person can also lead to becoming a controlling adult. If you had an overbearing or abusive parent, or if you came out of a relationship with a domineering or abusive partner, you may overcompensate for having had your life dictated by other people by going to the opposite extreme and seeking to control everything. You may believe that if you don't take control of the situation, someone else will. Some people approach work, friendships, and other relationships with the belief that there will always be winners and losers. They may think, *Someone has to run the show while everyone else gets run over, so if I don't want to get run over, then I have to be the one in charge.* They hold tightly to power because they believe they have to either control or be controlled.

People who are overwhelmed with too many roles and responsibilities may also become controlling. Since they have so much going on, they may feel that everything has to be finely orchestrated or the whole thing will fall apart. They may feel that they cannot risk letting someone else drop the ball, so they only trust themselves to handle everything. We need to be mindful of how we may be contributing to this dynamic by saying yes when we should be saying no because it's too much. Take a moment to think about what is at the foundation of any control issues that you might have—whether it's rooted in neglect, trauma, being dominated or controlled, or an overwhelming season of life. Ultimately, each of these issues is connected to fear—fear of what might happen if things don't go your way.

Certain events can also trigger control issues because people sometimes become more controlling when they're stressed. Those who are perfectionistic can be controlling because they want everything to be just so. For example, one spouse in a marriage may prefer that something around the house be done exactly their way, so that person becomes the only one who can do it. If that spouse doesn't have any flexibility around, say, how clothes should be folded, that spouse can become overwhelmed, angry, or resentful about doing the same task all the time because their partner won't do it the exact same way.

Interestingly, some people become more controlling when they are uncertain, because they don't want to appear weak or vulnerable. Rather than becoming more open to feedback and guidance, they double down on doing things their way because of their insecurity.

For many, controlling behavior is related to impatience. Anxiety and fear are also at the root of impatience, because we might worry that if we wait for other people to act, things will go badly; we'd rather jump in and take over.

THE COSTS OF CLINGING TO CONTROL

Some people take full ownership of the fact that they are controlling and experience no shame or regret about it. They might think, "Well, no, Dr. Thema, if you knew my family, or if you had my job, or if you went to my church, you would know why I have to take care of everything." Whatever the case may be, I want you to know that being controlling does come with costs. For one thing, you're probably exhausted. I understand on a personal and professional level what it feels like to carry the weight of the world on your shoulders. It is too much, even though you might not realize it, especially if you've lived your whole life this way. You may have grown up accustomed to never being able to take a breath or never experiencing joy or peace. You may feel constant obligations, duties, responsibilities, and pressures, but I want you to know that there is another way to live.

Often people who are controlling will stereotype those who choose to live differently: "Well, that's how lazy people live" or "That's for people who don't care or don't have a purpose in life." We don't have to operate at either extreme. We don't have to either do nothing with our lives or be controlling, driven, and perfectionistic. Rather, we can live a purposeful, motivated life while also balancing it with rest, joy, laughter, and fun.

Exhaustion has a psychological and physical effect on us. Our physical health suffers when we are too controlling and perfectionistic, and this can manifest in a variety of symptoms, so check in with yourself. Engaging in controlling behaviors can be driven by high stress and anxiety. Constant stress and anxiety can have negative consequences on your heart, blood pressure, sleep, nervous system, digestive system, and immune system. If you're saying that a fast pace of life suits you, does your body agree with you?

Not only is controlling behavior emotionally and physically draining, it also negatively affects your relationships and how people relate to you. It can lead to people avoiding you, ending the friendship, or staying silent in your presence. If they felt comfortable and safe enough, some of these people might let you know that you can be controlling. This kind of behavior affects your family, your friendships, and your romantic relationships. Being a controlling partner really causes the relationship to suffer and leads to a disconnect, even if it manifests itself in less obvious ways, like if the other person is silently checked out. For the sake of your health, relationships, and overall wellness, reflect on getting to a place of greater balance.

HOW TO RELEASE CONTROL ISSUES

When it comes to releasing control issues, the first thing I would recommend is relaxing, or as some might say, chilling out. You might be stressing everyone out with your level of intensity, so look for other outlets for your energy. I have clients who are more advanced in years and have never discovered their hobbies; they don't even know what they enjoy. No matter how old you are, now is a good time to find out what puts a smile on your face. Try different things: look up free events in your city, go to a concert, take a dance class, or just bop around in your living room if you'd prefer. Playing with your children or grandkids can help you come out of your shell, set aside any stuffiness or to-do lists, and find joy. I teach at Pepperdine University and tell my graduate students that if they're going to work with children, they'll have to get in touch with their joy. If they're too serious, kids will not be responsive to that; they'll just shut down and detach. Yes, there's a time and place to talk to kids about heavy issues, but we have to cultivate the ability to play, because that's also what we're trying to cultivate in children; we want to restore their joy if they've been through difficult circumstances. Whether you're twenty, forty, or sixty, now is a good time to restore your joy as well. When you're living from a more joyful place, you'll be less stressed and controlling, and you'll approach situations with greater ease.

I would also recommend delegating tasks and being willing to say no to some things. If you're always running the show, you'll never empower other people—including your coworkers, children, and spouse—to discover their own gifts and step up and shine. I invite you to think about one thing that you currently do and would be willing to delegate or share with someone else. We're not always aware of how we've taken over certain projects. Back when I was completing my doctoral program and interning,

I came up with an idea to start a poetry therapy group. I was so excited, and the director of the clinic assigned me a therapist to work with. After we ran the first session, that therapist came up to me and said, "So, Thema, we're supposed to do this together. What part do you want me to do?" I hadn't intentionally excluded her, but I was so focused on my vision for the project that I overlooked what she might have to offer. I then had to be very intentional to meet with her ahead of the next session to figure out how each of us would contribute to the project. As a result, the next session was much richer. All this is to say that whether it's on your radar, there is a cost to controlling behavior. It is causing you and others to miss out, so I invite you to consider: What are you willing to invite others to participate in? Where are you willing to step back so that other people can shine?

This is also an issue of setting boundaries. If feeling overwhelmed is contributing to your controlling behavior, you may be doing too much. Isn't that something? You're doing too much and micromanaging everything you're doing. What is it that you need to say no to so that you can live with greater ease?

Finally, I recommend challenging and shifting negative thoughts. You might believe that if you don't do everything, what results will be a disaster, or if others don't do everything the way you want them to, then that means they don't love or care about you. You might think that if you let go, you're going to be hurt, disappointed, or devastated, because no one else cares about those things the way you do. You might imagine catastrophes that keep you locked into the need for control. If you tend to overgeneralize with words like *all*, *no one*, or *everyone*, fear might be distorting the reality. Instead of saying "No one cares" or "No one will do the work," recognize the truth that there are some people who care and some who don't. If you let go of a task, someone else might do it differently, and that's okay. Alternatively, maybe no one will take up the task, and that is also okay, because it might not be needed in this season.

Walter is a married father of four. He sought counseling after his wife told him she is unhappy in the marriage because of his controlling behaviors. When he first came to see me, he was interpreting his wife's comments as some admission that she was seeing someone else. After he shared the way he constantly monitored her, it quickly became clear that his behavior was based in insecurity and entitlement. He shared that he has always selected women he felt were better-looking and smarter than him. He felt they reflected well on him and raised his social status. Unfortunately, once he won them over, he would spend the rest of the relationship fearing he would lose them. He would show up at her job not to truly express love but to scope out if any of her coworkers could be a threat. He would select her clothes. He would get angry when she went to brunch with her girlfriends, either texting her nonstop until she finally left the restaurant or even a few times showing up there. We explored the way his actions could actually lead to the very thing he feared: losing his wife. We began to help him take a walk in his wife's shoes. Instead of feeling loved and adored, his wife feels he doesn't care about her feelings, doesn't trust her, and thinks he needs to think for her. We also discovered that Walter does not have a life himself. He is threatened by her friends and her sister because he doesn't have friends and is disconnected from his siblings. He feels unworthy of her love because he has to work on loving himself and building a life that he enjoys. Walter has begun focusing more on himself. He doesn't know what he likes, so he is trying different hobbies and activities to find out what aligns with him. He has also developed a list of alternative explanations for when his wife can't call him right back. Instead of assuming the worst, he allows his mind to ponder neutral options. She and her sister may be talking, so she is not looking at her phone. She may be in a meeting at work instead of being seduced by a coworker. Walter regrets that he has created tension and unhappiness in his wife's life and is working to love her in a more open manner.

ACTIVATION EXERCISE: Monitor yourself to see if you are adding peace or adding stress to your loved ones' lives. I invite you to really apply yourself this week to cultivate joy, recognize when you are controlling people or situations, check in with yourself and release anxiety and fear when necessary, and let people be themselves without silencing them or giving them a script. There is freedom in that. If you have been trying to maintain control of everything for as long as you can remember, don't you think it's time to let yourself exhale? Give yourself that gift.

AFFIRMATION: If it aligns with you, rest your hands on your lap and say these words: "I love with open hands. I honor my loved ones. I trust that I do not have to carry the world on my shoulders."

IV.

CONCLUSION

17

NOURISH YOUR HEART: UPGRADE YOUR LIFE

Congratulations for completing *Matters of the Heart*. What a beautiful journey this has been. You have taken in so much information and hopefully have found ways to apply it to your life. I invite you to take a sacred pause, a moment to think about the deeper meaning of this season of your life. Reflect on what you have learned about yourself and your relationships. Reflect on the journey and rhythm of your heart as you give yourself grace, compassion, and appreciation.

This is a good moment to take a slow breath and another sacred pause. Being mindful and soulful about this present moment:

- Visualize the loving life you are creating and want to create. (Find your breath.)
- Picture your healed and healing heart. (Connect with your breath.)
- See yourself in communities of care, mutuality, and love. (Ease into breath.)

- Recognize yourself in a state of wholeness, sacredness. (Choose your breath.)
- There you are. (Free your breath.)

Claim your heart. Feel it. Honor it. Occupy it.

In the aftermath of heartbreak and heart-wounding, you are here to be your authentic, loving self. Reflect in this moment on the affirmation: "If it matters to my heart, it matters to me."

You are aligning your life, love, and relationships.

I want to offer you some closing considerations to empower you to continuously upgrade your love life:

1. *Start your day in love.* Create a loving ritual. You may want it to be an expression of love to your creator, your ancestors, yourself, your loved ones, or all living things. Before you begin working inside or outside the house, contemplate the way you want to immerse yourself in love. You may want to start the day by listening to a love song, a recorded self-affirmation, a sacred song, or nature sounds. You may want to start by speaking love to yourself aloud, praying a prayer of worship and praise, telling your beloved one thing you love about them, writing your children a love note to put in their backpacks or lunch boxes, journaling about what or who is in your heart and mind on this morning, or even writing or reading love poems. To start your day in love, you cannot set your alarm at the point you need to jump out of the bed. When you do this, you start the day in anxiety, stress, and even panic. Wake up a little earlier so you can begin the day in love. You may want to love yourself with some hot tea, a slow bubble bath, some easy stretching,

or a nature walk. You may want to love your partner with morning kisses, massage, words of appreciation, or love-making. The love practice may be the same daily or each day you can engage a different practice. Shape your day heart-led, openhearted, heartful.

2. *Get out in nature.* Phones, TVs, movies, computers, and gadgets can provide good entertainment and information, but they can also be major sources of distraction. Sometimes you can sabotage your relationships by comparing your partner to fictional characters and celebrities and comparing your relationship with relationships on television and in movies. Additionally, social media can provide nonstop distraction from your loved ones. You may regularly find yourselves sitting on the couch together, dining at a restaurant, or even lying in bed together while you're both on your phone scrolling social media. You may also engage in secretive inappropriate exchanges or "situationships" with people online. Whatever you think about your romantic or platonic relationships or your family connections, try to plan some time together away from devices and experiencing nature together. It can be as simple as sitting outside or going for a walk. If you have access, you may want to go to a park, a beach, a garden, a playground, a lake, or a mountain. Fresh air, uncluttered time, and the healing of our natural world can bring new life to you and your relationships. Instead of numbing out on devices, let your heart and breath come alive in nature. Reconnect with each other in the presence of the spacious beauty of nature. It can remind you of your priorities, values, and heart.

3. *Set boundaries to protect time with your loved ones.* Time is sacred. Your energy is sacred. Do not give all of yourself away to work and busyness. Do not neglect your beloved. Make the people you care about a priority. Carve out time to nourish your relationships. You don't want to end up with an impressive résumé but an empty heart. You don't want to be an outer success while your heart remains broken. By picking up and reading this book, you are saying your heart matters. Let your schedule reflect that it matters. Understandably, you may have lots on your plate for many reasons. The key is letting your loved ones know that they are a priority, not just with your words but with your actions. Protect time to speak with them and share space and time with them. Be intentional. Don't always give those closest to you the scraps of your life. Arrange your time in such a way that they know they matter to you. When I speak of time, I'm talking not just quantity but quality. Perhaps with your work schedule, you don't have endless hours to sit on the phone or to hang out every evening, but you can ensure that the time you have together is quality time. Be present when you're present. Be attentive and curious about your loved ones' lives, feelings, hopes, and concerns. Be honest and deliberate in your sharing as well. To say yes to your heart and to nourish your relationships, you will need to say no to some things. You want people you love to feel appreciated not taken for granted. Be intentional about planning and protecting your relational time. Take time to play together, rest together, travel together, and dream together. It will feed your relationship. If you don't have friends or a partner, you may want to invest time in finding and creating those connections. Reflect

on places you can go and activities you can do to come in contact with people with similar interests or values. Spend time making new connections, because your heart matters and relationships are a desire of yours that deserves to be watered.

4. *Own your part.* Any relationship—familial, romantic, or platonic—requires the cultivation and attention of both people. Often it is easier for us to judge what other people are doing wrong. As you attend to your heart, you can release being critic, judge, and juror and instead become more self-reflective. How are you contributing to the dynamic in your relationship? (I need to always note if you are in an abusive relationship, there is no part for you to own. There is no excuse or justification for abuse.) In nonabusive relationships, each person shapes the environment by the way in which they show up. Bear in mind how your expressions, emotions, words, and actions co-create a relational rhythm. If you want things to shift, it is not just about waiting for your partner, friend, or relative to shift. Explore ways that you may want to shift to aid in the progress of the relationship. Owning your part can include recognizing any ways you have contributed to the problem, apologizing, and maintaining a positive change of behavior. Owning your part can also mean taking initiative instead of always waiting for your friend, partner, or relative to make plans, to show affection, or to raise difficult issues that need to be addressed. You have a role in your relationships. Own it.

5. *Get creative.* While ritual can be stabilizing, routine can also dry out relationships. When you always do the same

thing, eat the same food, say the same thing, your relationship can begin to lose freshness, passion, and aliveness. Open your heart to new experiences. Think outside the box. Stretch yourself beyond your familiar activities. Look around to see what is happening in your city. Try to go somewhere or do something different together. You can also get creative together. Sing, dance, write poetry, paint, or redecorate your home together. Try to find new ways to express your care. Experiment. Explore. Let your heart open you.

6. *Affirm.* Be intentional about ensuring that your affirmations outnumber your complaints. While it is necessary to speak up and address difficulties, you must also develop your capacity and motivation to encourage, affirm, validate, and build up those whom you love. Give those you love compliments, thank-you notes, and both private and public praise. Do not leave people having to guess or hope that you care about them. Make your care explicit. Express your affirmation on special days such as birthdays and anniversaries, but also throughout the year. You may have not grown up hearing affirmation, so it may sound fake or awkward at first, but you can develop the habit. The more you affirm others (and yourself), the more natural it will feel. Let your words heal and uplift, especially those whom you love. Break out of silence and the idea that being loving is somehow weak or shameful. Using your voice to affirm your love is a remarkable gift for both the hearer and you the speaker.

7. *Engage in spiritual practices.* Having a spiritual connection can enhance your intimacy and also fortify you to

outlast difficult seasons. Whether you identify as spiritual, religious, or both, reflect on the last time you shared that part of your life journey with your friend or partner. It's great when a relationship is nourishing intellectually, emotionally, and sexually. You can upgrade your relationship by also interweaving aspects of your spiritual lives. This may look like praying, meditating, singing, attending services, volunteering, and even advocating for justice together. You may want to start the day reading a sacred text together and discussing it. You may want to journal at the end of the day about something that felt sacred to you that day and then share your responses with each other. Individually you can feed your soul, and in the presence of those you love, you can co-create soul food where everyone is nourished. Do the things that make your spirit come alive, and this will enhance and upgrade your life and your relationships.

8. *Have regular meetings.* Finally, I invite you to plan specific, regular conversations to upgrade your relationship. If you and your partner, friend, or relative are living together, you will bless yourselves by having regular business/finance meetings. You may benefit from discussing expenses, income, taxes, investments, savings, and future business plans. If all of you are informed and share your ideas, you will be working together instead of at odds regarding family financial goals. A meeting to address finances can also be a regular time to check in on the status of the relationship, including what is going well and what you still need from one another. A second type of meeting I recommend is therapy. You may say you all are doing fine, and that could well be true. The

reality is, you shouldn't wait for a crisis to go to couples therapy or family therapy. You can discuss unresolved issues, get to know each other better, and learn skills for handling conflict and stress. You can also learn ways to increase your emotional and sexual intimacy. If your partner or relative refuses to go to therapy, you can still go for yourself to heal your heart and determine your steps going forward. The final meeting I will mention is connecting with a larger community that is supportive and nourishing. This may be a friendship circle, a couples circle, your extended family, a walking group, a prayer group, or even a community service/advocacy group. Having the support of others can be helpful for encouragement, accountability, inspiration, and maintenance during difficult times.

Let's close this chapter with your success story.

My name is _____.
My heart wounds include _____.
A realization I had about my heart as I read this book is
_____. An action from this book
that I have used and will continue to use to activate love
in my life is _____. I know I can
have relationships that are _____.
I am worthy of _____. I'm proud of
myself for reading this book and for _____.
My heart is worthy of _____.

I'm excited about the healing and growing of your heart. I'm glad you invested time and energy into nourishing your relationship with yourself and others. I hope you are already seeing the fruits of your labor in relational improvements and upgrades. You're worthy of love, sacred love.

AFFIRMATION: If it aligns with you, place one hand on your heart and one hand on your belly as you say, "I welcome sacred love into my life. My heart is healing, opening, and expanding in beautiful ways. It is so."

ADDITIONAL RESOURCES

─────────

Bryant, Thema. *Homecoming: Overcome Fear and Trauma to Reclaim Your Whole, Authentic Self.* New York: TarcherPerigee, 2022.

Bryant, Thema. *Reclaim Yourself: The Homecoming Workbook.* New York: TarcherPerigee, 2024.

Buqué, Mariel. *Break the Cycle: A Guide to Healing Intergenerational Trauma.* New York: Dutton, 2024.

Delia, Lalah. *Vibrate Higher Daily: Live Your Power.* New York: HarperOne, 2019.

Elle, Alexandra. *After the Rain: Gentle Reminders for Healing, Courage, and Self-Love.* San Francisco: Chronicle Books, 2020.

John, Jaiya. *All These Rivers and You Chose Love.* Soul Water Rising, 2023.

Kolber, Aundi. *Try Softer: A Fresh Approach to Move Us Out of Anxiety, Stress, and Survival Mode—and into a Life of Connection and Joy.* Carol Stream, IL: Tyndale Refresh, 2020.

Levine, Amir, and Rachel Heller. *Attached: The New Science of Adult Attachment and How It Can Help You Find—and Keep—Love.* New York: TarcherPerigee, 2012.

Perry, Bruce D., and Oprah Winfrey. *What Happened to You?: Conversations on Trauma, Resilience, and Healing.* New York: Flatiron Books, 2021.

Tawwab, Nedra Glover. *Set Boundaries, Find Peace: A Guide to Reclaiming Yourself.* New York: TarcherPerigee, 2021.

Wolynn, Mark. *It Didn't Start with You: How Inherited Family Trauma Shapes Who We Are and How to End the Cycle.* New York: Penguin Life, 2016.

ACKNOWLEDGMENTS

Thank you, God, for the opportunity, gifts, and journey that have positioned me to offer these words. I am grateful to share what I have learned and continue to learn in head, heart, body, and soul. This life has been a miracle. My soul looks back and sees with clarity the way Divine Love has held and guided my heart.

Thank you to all who have been a part of the nourishing of my heart, especially the Gathering Sisters Ife, Ayo, Jamal, Amini, and Shavonne; Edith; Rosalynn; and my wonderful parents, Bishop John and Reverend Cecelia Bryant.

Thank you, J.J., for the gardening, marinating, and interweaving. Each heart ceremony has blessed me. May the next fifty yield the harvest our ancestors prayed for.

Many thanks to my literary agent, Chris Park, for being so much more than an agent. I am blessed by your support, guidance, and heart on this journey. Thank you for your consistent wisdom and care. I am so grateful to walk this journey with you.

Much appreciation to my incredible team at TarcherPerigee.

Thank you for believing in and honoring my voice. I am so grateful for the way you have valued my process and intentions from the beginning. I am enriched by your thoughtful team coming together with all your various gifts to amplify this healing work. Thank you for helping me to decolonize and disseminate psychology beyond the academy to make this knowledge accessible and engaging to people from all walks of life.

With the gift that each soul brings to my life, I am living the dream. Eyes open. Heart open. Arms open. And so it is. Amen.

ABOUT THE AUTHOR

Dr. Thema Bryant is author of the bestselling book *Homecoming: Overcome Fear and Trauma to Reclaim Your Whole, Authentic Self.* She is a licensed clinical psychologist, a third-generation ordained minister, and a sacred artist specializing in spoken word and dance. She is a tenured professor of psychology at Pepperdine University and the 2023 president of the American Psychological Association. Dr. Thema, as she is affectionately known, is a former psychology representative to the United Nations and past president of the Society for the Psychology of Women. She completed her doctoral training at Duke University and her postdoctoral training at Harvard Medical Center. She is a favorite among media psychologists and raises awareness about liberation psychology and mental health on social media and through her *Homecoming Podcast.* Dr. Thema is the mother of Ife and Ayo, whose names mean Love and Joy.

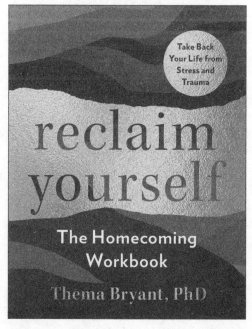